Not Bloody Likely

The Shaw Festival: 1962-1973

Production photographs by Robert C. Ragsdale, A.R.P.S., M.P.A.
Ludvik Dittrich, Lorne Blunt, Helen Flaherty

Not Bloody Likely

The Shaw Festival: 1962-1973

Text by Brian Doherty

J. M. Dent & Sons (Canada) Limited

ISBN 0-460-93648-4

Printed and bound in Canada by The Bryant Press Limited

PHOTOGRAPHS

The publishers are grateful to the following for permission to reproduce photographs.

ACTRA, Toronto, page 160, photograph of Barry Morse by Manning Wilson, London.
Artrex, Niagara-on-the-Lake, pages 108, 109; page 160, photograph of Brian Doherty.
Lorne Blunt, Toronto, pages 24-27.
Tom Bochsler, Hamilton, pages 128-133.
Canadian Broadcasting Corporation-Société Radio-Canada, Toronto, page 160, photograph of Andrew Allan.
Robert Dawson, Dublin, page 76, photograph of Micheál MacLiammóir.
Ludvik Dittrich, Scarborough, pages 84-85, 88-89 centre, 95-97, 100-103, 114-115, 146-147.
Gino Empry Public Relations, Toronto, page 160, photograph of Sean Mulcahy.
Helen Flaherty, Ottawa, pages 118, 121 right.
Morley Fleming, Niagara-on-the-Lake, page 137 right.
Preston Haskell, St Catharines, page 160, photograph of Raymond Wickens.
Dr Donald Mason, page 113.
Robert C . Ragsdale, A.R.P.S., M.P.A. Toronto, pages 23, 28-41, 46-49, 50 bottom, 51-53, 62-75, 77-83, 86-87, 88 left, 89 right, 90-94, 98-99, 104-107, 116-117, 119, 120, 120-121 centre, 122-123, 125, 126, 135 bottom, 139, 140-145, 148-151, 160, photographs of Muriel Sherrin, Calvin Rand, Judith Hendry.
Ron Roels, Niagara Falls, Ontario, page 136 left, top and bottom.
The St Catharines Standard, Bev Christensen, pages 134, 135 top, 136-137; Mike Conley, page 138 bottom; Les Slorach, page 138 top.
Michael Shane, page 160, photograph of Thomas Burrows.
The Thom Partnership Architects/Planners, Toronto, pages 2-3, from a water colour by R. Kovach; pages 60-61.
The Vancouver Sun, page 160, photograph of Paxton Whitehead.
The Weir Foundation, Epstein bust of Shaw, page 6.

PREFACE

'Not bloody likely!' was Eliza Doolittle's shocking retort when at the climax of Act III of *Pygmalion*, after her début as a *real lady*, she was asked if she intended to walk home. For me, Eliza's outburst is filled with a very personal significance. Let me explain why.

During the struggling early years of the Shaw Festival, when my Niagara-on-the-Lake friend and neighbour Calvin Rand and I were appealing to everyone—friends and strangers, the public at large—for support for the Shaw Festival, it was Eliza's phrase, or some equally emphatic variation of it, that was the most frequent response to our appeals. But as Calvin and I and our loyal disciples persevered, refusing to be discouraged, the phrase took on a different tone for us. Eliza's fiery words became our battle cry in the struggle against the Philistines. Would we give up the fight for a Shaw Festival? Not bloody likely!

What follows is a personal chronicle of those years of effort and achievement. Others will write the story with greater skill and objectivity, but no one will do the job with greater love and gratitude.

'Clontarf'
New Year's day 1974   *Brian Doherty*

SHAW IN CANADA

Why Shaw? Or, more specifically, why did I, along with the others who took the initiative in bringing the Shaw Festival into existence, select George Bernard Shaw as the playwright at the core of our theatrical dream? That is the question that journalists, radio and television interviewers, and even curious playgoers often ask me.

There is, of course, an easy, ready answer. It's simply that Shaw was the only outstanding playwright writing in English, with the obvious exception of Shakespeare, who produced a sufficient number of plays to support a festival. Other dramatists have written fine plays that have endured. I think of Ben Jonson, for example, of Marlowe, Webster, Congreve, Goldsmith, Sheridan, Wilde, Pinero, Barrie, Maugham, and O'Casey, not to mention the American Eugene O'Neill. But it seemed to me that none of those men had produced enough truly great works to inspire a successful and continuing festival. Shaw, on the other hand, wrote about thirty full-length plays, including *Back to Methuselah*, which is as long as three or four conventional plays, as well as some twenty shorter pieces, several of which play for more than an hour. So there it was, a formidable body of fifty possible productions, certainly enough to sustain a festival.

That is the ready answer. However, the more I pondered the question—Why Shaw?—the more I understood that there was for me a much more deeply rooted answer. I became aware of just how great an influence Shaw had exerted on me through all the long years I had worshipped at his shrine. I realize now that by the time we made the decision in favour of Shaw in 1962, I had come to consider him not only a great playwright but also a great prophet of the twentieth century.

Historically, going back now to a time long before I got into the theatre in the 1930s, Canadians were slow to appreciate Shaw. At the turn of the century British theatre critics and audiences raged in bitter controversy over Shaw and his fellow non-conformist Henrik Ibsen, but Canadians were largely unaware of the controversy. Their taste in theatre ran to bowdlerized versions of Shakespeare's best-known plays and to sentimental romances like *Uncle Tom's Cabin, East Lynne,* and *Human Hearts.*

Before the First World War, a few British and American companies, of widely varying merit, ventured on tour into Canada. Some even featured celebrated performers: Maude Adams, Mrs Patrick Campbell, Henry Irving, Ellen Terry, and Sarah Bernhardt. But, celebrated performers or not, woe betide the touring company that failed to cater to the Canadian taste for wholesome theatre fare. Mrs Patrick Campbell, despite her fame and beauty, found herself denounced in Toronto in 1903 when she dared to appear in *The Second Mrs Tanqueray.* To the disgust of staid Torontonians, Paula Tanqueray was that most shocking of all creatures, 'a woman with a past'.

'A good woman is a dramatic impossibility,' stormed Mrs Campbell on that occasion. She was later to play Eliza Doolittle in the original production of *Pygmalion,* and appropriately enough, to be the first to utter those shocking words, 'Not bloody likely!'

As Murray D. Edwards has recorded in his book on English-language theatre in Eastern Canada from the 1790s to 1914, *A Stage in Our Past*, Shaw made his Canadian theatrical début on Christmas Eve 1904. The place was Winnipeg, the play was *Candida,* and the producer was a young American, Lester Lonergan, who also played Marchbanks. Oddly enough the Canadian première came in the same year as the first London production of *Candida.* One reaction to the play is to be found in the review of C. W.

Handscomb, the fire-breathing drama critic of the *Manitoba Free Press*, a man who earlier in the year had denounced Ibsen's *Ghosts* as 'just plain smut'. His comments on *Candida* were less vitriolic, and in fact, he seemed more confused than hostile.

'Why, this chap, Shaw, seems bent on puzzling us,' Handscomb wrote. 'Indeed puzzle and paradox constitute the very kernel of the nut he gives us to crack. *Candida* may be serious in motive, the philosophy of a genius, or it may be just the brilliant buncombe of a jesting cynic without any underlying purpose.'

Next came *Man and Superman* in Montreal on January 21, 1907. Montreal was just one stop along the way for a touring company that starred Robert Loraine, one of England's finest actors of the day. The play proved a great hit for Shaw and for Loraine in every city on its North American tour, but it was presented without Act III, the long and controversial 'Hell Scene'. I wonder what the public reaction would have been had the 'Hell Scene' been included.

Perhaps it would have been closer to the reception that Winnipeg gave a few months later to the first production in Canada of *Mrs Warren's Profession*. The American première of this remarkable play had caused a great stir. The notion that the affluent and apparently respectable Mrs Warren operated a string of brothels was too much for the authorities, who closed the play and arrested the cast for indecency. The theatregoers of Winnipeg, attracted by the scandalous reports, turned out in large numbers to see a production of the play offered by Rose Coghlan, an American actress well known for her performances in conventional repertoire. Did the Winnipeg audience react with shock and dismay? Quite the contrary. They received *Mrs Warren's Profession*, amazingly enough, with yawns and puzzled looks. Only the redoubtable C. W. Handscomb rose to the occasion. 'Unwholesome . . . repulsive . . . sewerlike . . . meretricious glitter . . . beatification of evil living' were his descriptions.

Poor, brave Rose Coghlan! She quickly returned to her popular portrayal of Lady Teazle and to leading roles in more acceptable vehicles like *The Silver King* and *Diplomacy*. Poor Shaw—a genius laying bare the truth decades before the world was ready to accept it. *Mrs Warren's Profession* was not produced publicly in England until 1925, thirty-two years after Shaw wrote it. Now, of course, the play is accepted as one of his early masterpieces.

A month after Rose Coghlan's disaster, Shaw's first play, *Widowers' Houses*, ran into another wall of indifference in Toronto. Miss Effie Shannon, an American actress who was at the beginning of what was to be a long and distinguished career, starred in the play at the Princess Theatre. One Toronto critic, who had nothing but praise for Miss Shannon and the rest of the cast, found the play itself 'tiresome and boring'. So did Torontonians, who generally ignored the production.

The year 1907 was a busy one for Shaw in Canada. Audiences may have stayed away, and critics may have continued to carp, but at least the Shaw plays were being produced. Johnston Forbes-Robertson, a noted English actor, arrived in Toronto in 1907 with *Caesar and Cleopatra* and played to excellent notices. So did the renowned Ellen Terry in a 1907 production of *Captain Brassbound's Conversion* in Montreal. As usual, though, the critics dismissed Shaw as a boring creator of puppets. No justice yet for Shaw.

Candida returned to Canada in 1913, this time to the Russell Theatre in Ottawa, and it was to be the last Shaw production in Canada until after the First World War. The play was produced by Miss A. E. Horniman, who played the title role. Miss Horniman was one of the most important influences on British theatre in the early decades of this century. Her influence unfortunately did not extend to the Ottawa critics and audiences. *Candida* met the same fate as most of the other Shaw plays in pre-1914 Canada: lots of praise for the performers, none at all for the author.

After the First World War, Shaw and I arrived at the Hart House

Theatre in Toronto at about the same time. Shaw's plays made up a regular part of that dynamic theatre's repertoire. It was typical of its enlightened play policy that Hart House was probably the first (and perhaps the only) North American company to present Shaw's *The Shewing-up of Blanco Posnet*, an unusual Midwestern drama. Among the standard Shaw works offered were *Misalliance* (1924), *Great Catherine* and *Heartbreak House* (both in 1926, the latter as a Canadian première), *The Man of Destiny* (1927), *How He Lied to Her Husband* (1927), *The Doctor's Dilemma* (1927), *Major Barbara* (1931), and *The Devil's Disciple* (1934). To me the memories of those productions are pure joy.

So, too, are the memories of the British companies led to Canada by Maurice Colbourne and Barry Jones. Beginning in 1928, they went on tour with troupes of first-rate actors. Over several seasons they brought to Canada productions of *You Never Can Tell, John Bull's Other Island, The Philanderer, The Doctor's Dilemma, Fanny's First Play, Candida, Arms and the Man, Man and Superman,* and *The Apple Cart.* I saw many of the plays at the Royal Alexandra Theatre in Toronto.

The Colbourne-Jones company returned for one last tour in 1939, shortly after the outbreak of the Second World War. Unhappily the tour was a failure, and I recall Colbourne's pessimism in a conversation I had with him. He told me that he had doubts about Canada's theatrical future. The audiences, he complained, were small and uneducated to drama, and the theatres were wretched. Colbourne painted a gloomy picture.

During and after the Second World War, American touring companies brought productions of Shaw plays to Canada. I remember particularly Gertrude Lawrence in *Pygmalion* and Katharine Cornell in *Candida* and in *The Doctor's Dilemma,* with Raymond Massey. The success of these visiting companies convinced me that Shaw the playwright was far from dead as far as Canadian audiences were concerned. From that time on I began to explore the idea of a Shavian theatre in our country.

SHAW IN THE COURT HOUSE

The long period when Shaw's plays were offered only sporadically in Canada, by touring companies or by determined local theatre groups, came to an end with the conception in 1962 of Niagara-on-the-Lake's Shaw Festival. And the Festival, for its part, experienced its first faint twinges of life on a cold February evening of that year.

My friend Jean Marsh had invited a small group of us, including a New York actress, to her flat in Niagara-on-the-Lake for after-dinner coffee and drinks. Gathered round the fire we chatted. Soon all of us were absorbed in our favourite topic: the beauty and charm of Niagara-on-the-Lake and the fact that its historic heritage was being threatened.

'Let's do something,' I said at one point in the long evening of talk. 'Instead of worrying and criticizing, let's do something for the town we love, something we believe in.'

'How about theatre?' It was the New York actress who made that suggestion.

'Shaw!' I suddenly exclaimed. After all those years of gestation, the idea seemed to explode in my head. 'Shaw. Shaw would be wonderful.'

I started to build on the notion: 'We'd have to make it really professional, something like Shakespeare in Stratford. We couldn't be just another summer stock company. It would have to be more than that.'

'But where in the world would we stage it?' someone sensibly asked.

The historic nineteenth-century Court House came immediately to mind. It had disadvantages, plenty of them, but it was centrally placed, right on the main street, and it had an atmosphere of quiet charm. When we broke up that night, I had agreed to explore all possibilities, to organize a small committee, and to call a formal meeting.

Next day at my law office, I began to come down to earth. Was the Shaw project a pipe dream? The senior partner of my firm thought I would be mad to take on still one more outside chore. In the light of day the idea did seem impractical: we had no money and very few experienced people. Why not forget it?

Just as I was on the verge of abandoning the project, mentally at any rate, one of the previous evening's enthusiasts called me to say that she had arranged for us to use the Court House for an exploratory meeting. Would I serve as chairman? Yes, by God, I would. And with that decision I launched my new double life: law by day, theatre by night. It was the beginning of my impossible dream, a dream that at times turned into a nightmare, but a dream that finally came true on June 12, 1973, with the opening of the new Shaw Festival Theatre.

To go back to that first meeting in the Court House in 1962, about forty people showed up. Some were definitely doubting Thomases, but the majority radiated enthusiasm. And in the old Court Room of mid-Victorian design, with its imposing heraldic shield, we resolved to go ahead. The meeting named me producer and artistic director. Now I had the titles, but there was something I didn't have: money. The treasury was empty.

First I did a little recruiting. I persuaded Maynard Burgess, an actor-director in Niagara Falls, New York, to join us for the first season. (Fittingly enough Maynard was to return to us in the 1973 inaugural season for a part in *Fanny's First Play*.) Then I brought my neighbour into the project. Calvin Rand is an educator and man of the arts, who was at that time teaching English at the University of Buffalo. For several generations the Rand family had summered at their estate in Niagara-on-the-Lake.

When I first approached Calvin, he was just a neighbour, but as we worked together I grew more and more impressed with his character, his wide-ranging mind, and his sincere love of Niagara-on-the-Lake. Down through the years he became a friend, who took on many difficult jobs for the Festival and in 1965 replaced me as its president.

Right from the start we had a few strong and able supporters who dedicated themselves behind the scenes to business and public relations, advertising and subscriptions: Jean Marsh, Bas and Jean Mason, Lillian Magder, Barbara Tranter, Marion Roach, Pat Rand, and Dorothy Middleditch who remains a member of our executive to this day. If there's one lesson I've learned over the years, it's that almost anything is possible for a project with a strong volunteer committee.

Maynard Burgess and I set about choosing two Shaw plays for our first season. We finally decided on *Candida* and the 'Hell Scene' from *Man and Superman*. Both had the advantages for our company, nearly penniless as it was, of requiring only one set and a small cast. We made a few other basic decisions: no one—actor, director, or offstage worker—was to be paid a salary. We dubbed the enterprise 'Salute to Shaw' and announced a season of four weekends between June 29 and August 11.

Now came the problem of casting the plays. We were lucky to find David Loveless and Mavis Corser, recent arrivals from England who had had amateur acting experience. David was cast as Don Juan and Mavis as Doña Ana. Eric Davis of the Welland Little Theatre was cast as the Statue, and Maynard Burgess, as well as directing, was to play the Devil. We decided to stage the play as a reading, as Charles Laughton had done. This method suited our enterprise very well, for not only was it stylish, but it demanded no more in the way of a set than drapes, lecterns, and simple lighting.

We called rehearsals for the Court House South Hall, and we began with the 'Hell Scene'. While the players rehearsed, the rest of us went into

15

action on publicity and promotion. The *Niagara Advance,* the *Niagara Evening Review,* the *Welland Tribune,* and the *Niagara Falls Gazette* were all very co-operative in printing our advance publicity, including stories I pounded out at night on my ancient Remington. Perhaps our biggest publicity break came from Betty Lampard, the drama critic for the *St Catharines Standard,* who through the years has helped the Festival tremendously with her articles and reviews.

Finally our first opening night arrived, Friday June 29. It couldn't have been a more appropriate occasion to stage the 'Hell Scene': the town was in the grip of a heat wave. The Court House, despite its high ceilings and stone walls, was a furnace—torture for actors and audience alike.

In an attempt to ease the situation, Dorothy Middleditch, Calvin Rand, and I ran up and down Queen Street begging and borrowing electric fans, which we scattered round the auditorium. The fans helped very little.

I've been through many nerve-wracking opening nights, but I doubt if any could match that sweltering evening in the Court House. Besides the heat, there were plenty of other handicaps: the flat floors with no elevations, the miserably small stage with no wings or flies, the uncomfortable stacking chairs. There seemed no end of torments.

In spite of the drawbacks, an excellent house of nearly two hundred people stayed to the end, and they liked the show. Laughter and applause echoed through the Court House. What's more, they all expressed interest in our next play.

Maynard Burgess assembled his cast for *Candida*: Barbara Ransom, Jean Malloy, Tim Devlin, Terry Cahill, Edward Fordham, and David Michener. Rehearsals were called for the week after the first opening. Alice Crawley, a gifted professional painter, created an authentic late-Victorian setting, dressed with equally authentic furnishings borrowed from mansions in town. Louis Berai, a well-known dress designer enhanced the set with excellent period costumes.

Another opening night, another success. *Candida*, performed for the first time on July 27, drew an even larger audience than the 'Hell Scene'. The crowd was enthusiastic, and Betty Lampard gave us a large and flattering spread in the *St Catharines Standard*. The Buffalo, Toronto, and Hamilton critics hadn't noticed us, nor had any government fund-granting body, but we were satisfied. We had mounted productions of Shaw that had engaged us and the audiences as well.

Before the second season, we had to make a crucial decision. Should we proceed on a professional basis? It was a risky proposition, but if we expected to progress artistically, to improve our theatre facilities, and to put the Festival on a solid foundation, it was the only choice.

That decision raised two immediate problems: to find a first-rate artistic director and to raise the money to pay him and all the other professionals he would expect to sign for the second season.

I undertook the first chore, and for many weeks of that fall and winter it was discouraging work. The right people turned out to be either not available or not interested. And who could blame them? Few theatre people had even heard of that group of Shaw enthusiasts in Niagara-on-the-Lake. Then the ever-resourceful actress Jane Mallett gave me the suggestion I needed.

'Why, I know just the man you're looking for,' she said. 'Andrew Allan!'

Of course. I had admired Andrew's work for many years, particularly his brilliant radio drama productions for the CBC. When Jane offered to bring us together to explore a possible working relationship, I leaped at the chance. A few days later Andrew and I sat down at his favourite wining and dining spot, the Celebrity Club.

Andrew impressed me deeply. He was intelligent and knowledgeable. He told me that he had grown disenchanted with television and that theatre was his first love. That statement endeared him to me.

Then he admitted that he was as keen about doing Shaw as I was. I needed no more encouragement. I offered him the job of artistic director of the Shaw Festival, and he accepted it, providing he could have the assistance of his friend, actor-director Sean Mulcahy. I drove home from our meeting in a buoyant mood—I'd found my man!

Now to finances. We had two professional directors and would be employing professional actors. How were we going to pay them, even though they were prepared to work for minimum salaries? A number of Niagara-on-the-Lake businessmen and theatre-minded residents had been very generous with donations, but we were far short of our proposed budget. At precisely that worrying point, my friend Mavor Moore telephoned me from Toronto.

'Are you interested in booking a pre-Toronto engagement of this year's *Spring Thaw?*' he asked me.

Mavor's offer came like an answer to our prayers. We took it up on terms that could net us a thousand dollars. Our committee went right into action and sold enough tickets to guarantee a full house. When the evening was over, we had banked enough money to launch our critical 1963 season.

There were three Andrew Allan years at the Shaw Festival: 1963, 1964, and 1965. In a dozen ways, large and small, those seasons set the pace, and set some standards as well for events and ideas, for patterns of growth and direction, that were to characterize the Festival through the following years of its remarkable growth.

Andrew Allan heralded expansion in many directions. His first season was three weeks long—a significant increase from the eight performances of the initial year. His second season was extended to four weeks and his third to six weeks. In the beginning there was a pronounced atmosphere of make-do. Since funds were too limited to permit the rental of office space, most of the business of the Festival was conducted from my home. We had no workshop, and Martha Mann, who was engaged as

designer for the 1963 season, cheerfully built and painted sets in a parking
lot behind the Town Hall. Necessity often led to inspired improvisation. As
Andrew grew more and more frustrated by the confining dimensions of the
small stage, he hit on the ingenious notion of converting the old Court
House doors on either side of the stage into exits and entrances for the
actors, thereby enlarging and enhancing the performing area.

But the Allan years were marked as well by a growing sense of
professionalism. The acting community became more aware of the high
standards the Festival set for itself, and many Canadian theatre people of
the first rank joined the Festival company. Several performers who made
their first appearances at the Shaw Festival during the Allan years were to
return year after year. Betty Leighton, who was the charming Lady
Utterword of the 1964 production of *Heartbreak House,* is one example. In the
same year two designers joined the company: Lawrence Schafer and
Donald Acaster, who created and produced sets and lighting of a calibre that
matched the growing excellence of the performances.

During the 1963 season, the Shaw Festival established a board of
directors and was incorporated as a non-profit organization. That step made
us eligible for tax-free grants and donations. While individuals were
generous with their contributions, it was to be a while before any large sums
of money materialized. In fact, it was not until 1965 that the Shaw Festival
received its first government grant, in the amount of $10,000, from the
Ontario Arts Council. Until now we had been augmenting box office
receipts with bank loans guaranteed by members of the Board. That $10,000
grant enabled us to wipe out all outstanding debts. From that day to this,
the Shaw Festival has operated entirely in the black—surely setting a record
among theatrical companies. Grants and donations added to box office
receipts have been sufficient to cover the growing annual budgets.

Meanwhile, other seeds, which were to grow and blossom, were
being sown. In 1965 the Shaw Seminar was founded, in co-operation with

Brock University. I had the satisfying task of serving as its chairman. From a first small gathering in 1965, the Seminar has grown to an annual conference that brings together Shavian scholars, critics, and theatre devotees to discuss and shed closer light on Shaw and his works.

That year, 1965, saw the first presentation at the Festival of a non-Shavian play. It was Sean O'Casey's *The Shadow of a Gunman,* which was to be followed in later years by other plays written by the best of Shaw's contemporaries. This we felt, and I think justly, was a policy that would enhance the Festival repertoire and at the same time place Shaw himself in a clearer perspective.

Not all the signs in the Allan years were promising, however. On the negative side there was the indifference demonstrated by some of the local residents toward both the plays and the players. Not a serious matter in itself perhaps, but one that signalled difficulties later on when the Festival began its serious search for a site on which to build a permanent theatre. Much as we loved the charming Court House, its facilities were plainly inadequate.

At first, both players and audience accepted the Court House in the familiar spirit of make-do. Improvements to the old building helped: air conditioning and an expanded apron in 1963, elevated seating in 1964. But as early as the second season, we began casting about for a roomier, more comfortable theatre. Briefly the Brock Cinema was considered; it was just down the street from the Court House. When we discovered how much it would cost for repairs and remodelling, we quickly abandoned that idea. Then Ed Mirvish suggested that the Shaw Festival might be held at his Royal Alexandra Theatre in Toronto, but we were by now persuaded that the Festival and Niagara-on-the-Lake belonged together. And so the search went on.

At least it proceeded from a position of strength and confidence. In 1965 Ray Wickens was engaged as the first full-time company manager and director of publicity. He brought continuity of a more tangible sort—the continuity of business going forward day by day, now in a store front on Queen Street, just a few doors away from the Court House. In that same year the Festival Board was solidified under three men: Calvin Rand became president; Dr Bill Blue, a neuro-surgeon from St Catharines who had been sympathetic to the aims of the Festival from the beginning (even to the extent of doing walk-on roles in some of the productions) became vice-president; and Peter Brown became treasurer.

The Festival drew strength as well from the spreading recognition it achieved during Andrew Allan's tenure as artistic director. With each succeeding season, the audiences grew (grew so quickly, in fact, that as early as 1964 we had to increase the number of ticket outlets to keep pace with the advance demand for tickets). And critical recognition grew as well. Now each opening night attracted critics from the major newspapers of the Niagara peninsula, Buffalo, and Toronto.

Andrew Allan voiced his thoughts about his first season at the Shaw Festival in the 1964 Winter-Spring issue of *The Performing Arts in Canada*.

DRAMA IN THE COURT HOUSE

Bernard Shaw, as playwright, had to wait a long time before he broke through to the public. West End managers and West End critics found no beauty in him that they should desire him. Fringe productions by amateurs attracted few but Fabians. And when he did break through to a quite surprising success, he still found himself taken oddly.

'He is a merry preacher,' said the pontifical Arthur Symons, 'a petulant critic, a great talker. It is partly because he is an Irishman that he has transplanted the art of talking to the soil of the stage: Sheridan, Wilde, Shaw, our only modern comedians, all Irishmen, all talkers. It is by his astonishing skill of saying everything that comes into his head, with a spirit really intoxicating, that Mr Shaw has succeeded in holding the stage with undramatic plays, in which there is neither life nor beauty. . . . But those who amuse the world, no matter by what means, have their place in the world at any given moment. Mr Shaw is a clock striking the hour.'

The clock in the tower of the 1847 Court House at Niagara-on-the-Lake, Ontario, last summer struck many illuminating hours with the help of Mr Shaw—two score of years after Mr Symons' pronouncement.

The occasion was the 1963 Shaw Festival, produced by Brian Doherty, and in which I, as director, was associated with my fellow director, Sean Mulcahy, and an admirable company of Equity players from Toronto, Montreal, St Catharines, and Buffalo. We discovered together, if we had not known it before, that there was life in Bernard Shaw in 1963—and beauty, too, for that matter. And the ninety-five per cent audience we attracted to the Niagara Peninsula indicated that the public enjoyed sharing our discovery.

At the turn of the century even Shaw's good friend, William Archer, was begging the Irishman to 'repress his irrelevant whimsicality', to 'try to clothe his character-conceptions in flesh and blood, and realize the difference between knowingness and knowledge'. Archer need not have worried. His red-bearded friend was doing a great deal better in the flesh-and-blood department than most of his contemporaries imagined. We find that out when we play him today. Play him as flesh and blood, not as whimsicality and talk, and you'll find out how much exuberant humanity there is in the man. Shaw is the very antidote to despair.

Never downhearted or ruffled, Shaw in 1911 was amused by '. . . those critics and playgoers who are so obsessed by my strained legendary reputation that they approach my plays in a condition which is really one of derangement, and are quite unable to conceive a play of mine as anything but a trap baited with paradoxes, and designed to compass their ethical perversion and intellectual confusion'.

Well, things have happened since 1911. Shaw breaks through more clearly now. The young people of today find him much more their contemporary than Symons and Archer ever did.

At Niagara-on-the-Lake . . . we performed three bills: *You Never Can Tell*, a double bill of *How He Lied to Her Husband* and *The Man of Destiny*, and finally *Androcles and the Lion*. I had the privilege of directing the first two bills, Mr Mulcahy the third. Since he had played Valentine in *You Never Can Tell*, I felt it only fair to play the Roman Emperor in *Androcles*. These plays were written before the First World War; but, except for the costumes and the social *mores* (which were having the Shavian treatment anyway) none of our audiences found them to be bygone. . . .

The money that was raised to finance the venture was raised throughout the Niagara country and on both sides of the border. There is a healthy air about the place and the people and about the way things are done. Anyone anywhere who feels that a living theatre brings life to a community can get sweet breath from Niagara. And from Bernard Shaw, too.

The Court House, the first home of the Shaw Festival, opposite the Clock Tower on ▷ Queen Street in Niagara-on-the-Lake

1 9 6 3

James Edmond as Teddy, Michael Tabbitt as Henry, Denise Ferguson as Aurora

THE MAN OF DESTINY

*Guy Sanvido as Giuseppe, Ian
Thorne as Napoleon*

*James Beggs as the Sub-Lieutenant,
Guy Sanvido as Giuseppe, Margaret
Griffin as the Strange Lady, Ian
Thorne as Napoleon*

. . . Beggs was brilliant, turning in one of his best performances yet . . . without speaking a word. Starting with excellent make-up of mane, tail and those padded paws, he assembled a most plausible-yet-personable lion, half realistic rumbling and rippling tension, half winsome charm and cute capers. This was the best lion I've sighted since Bert Lahr. . . .

. . . Beggs came close to being skinned by the equally majestic Mr. Rodriguez (who has one of the noblest heads this side of ancient Athens), in the role of the brawny, brawling near-martyr, Ferrovius. . . .

. . . Almost miraculously, Miss Ferguson managed to blend ethereal grace with auburn allure to create a woman of instinctive, but not irrevocable chastity. . . .

Ron Evans, *The Telegram*, Toronto

James Beggs as the Lion

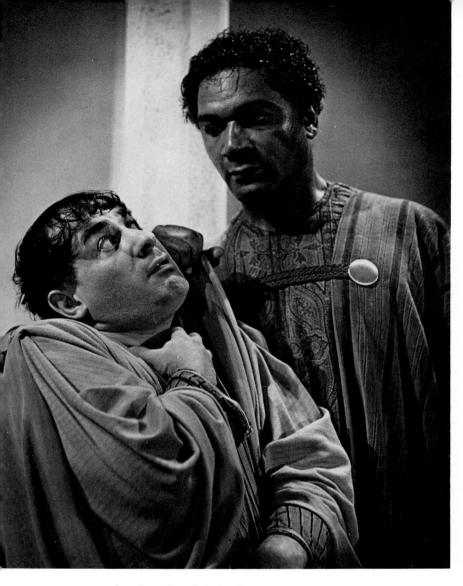

*Guy Sanvido as Spintho, Percy
Rodriguez as Ferrovius*

*Denise Ferguson as Lavinia,
Ian Thorne as the Captain*

*Norman Welsh as Captain Shotover, Mary
Benning as Ellie Dunn*

29

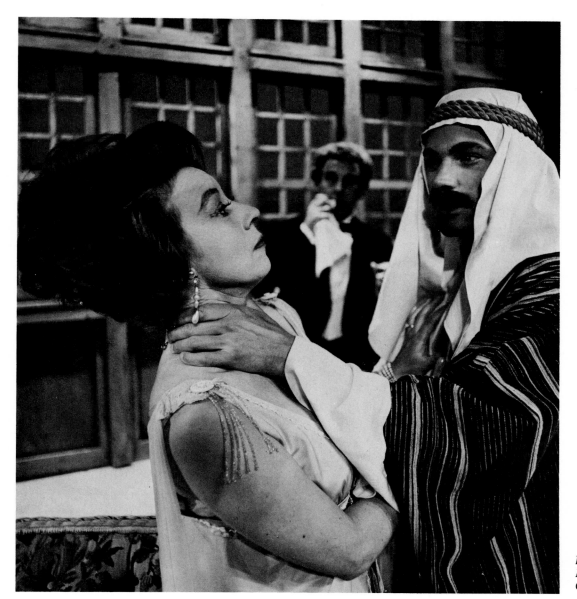

Betty Leighton as Lady Utterword,
Michael Tabbitt as Randall Utterword,
Christopher Newton as Hector Hushabye

Linda Livingston as Miss 'Z', Christopher Newton as Mr 'A'

THE DARK LADY OF THE SONNETS

Donald Ewer as the Beefeater, Jack Medley as William Shakespear

Moya Fenwick as Queen Elizabeth I, Linda Livingston as the Dark Lady

. . . It [*The Dark Lady of the Sonnets*] demands briskness in the direction and panache in the playing. It gets both, the former from Sean Mulcahy, the latter from Donald Ewer as the Beefeater, Jack Medley as Shakespear, Moya Fenwick as Elizabeth I, and Linda Livingston as Mary Fitton, the Dark Lady with whom Shakespear had planned to keep a tryst. . . .

David Cobb, *The Toronto Star*

JOHN BULL'S OTHER ISLAND

Sean Mulcahy as Larry Doyle, Paul Craig as Tom Broadbent, Leo Leyden as Matthew Haffigan

33

Gerard Parkes as Peter Keegan, Joyce Campion as Aunt Judy, Mary Benning as Nora Reilly

Alfred Gallagher as Colonel Pickering,
Paul Craig as Henry Higgins

Betty Leighton as Mrs Pearce, Gerard
Parkes as Alfred Doolittle

Jean Stainer as the Parlourmaid, Juliana
Saxton as Mrs Higgins

Paul Craig as Henry Higgins, Anne Butler as Eliza Doolittle

THE SHADOW OF A GUNMAN
Sean O'Casey

Lawrence Beattie as Adolphus Grigson,
Sean Mulcahy as Donal Davoren

Joyce Campion as Mrs Grigson, Gerard
Parkes as Seumas Shields

. . . Sean Mulcahy has given The
Shadow of a Gunman an excellent
Canadian debut production. . . .

His production plumps heavily for
vaudevillian comedy and so succeeds
splendidly.

Of course, he's aided immeasurably
by a fine cast, led by Mr. Parkes as the
roaring, grumbling, stammering
Seumas. This is a performance larger
than life, as befits the epic, hypocritical
braggart, and Mr. Mulcahy himself has
his best moments in the furious,
two-fisted scenes with his co-star. . . .
Ron Evans, *The Telegram*, Toronto

Nuala Fitzgerald as Minnie Powell,
Michael Snow as Tommy Owens, Alfred
Gallagher as Mr Gallogher, Marie Pringle
as Mrs Henderson, Sean Mulcahy as
Donal Davoren

Michael Snow as the Sweatshop Man,
Betty Leighton as the Sweatshop Woman

Anne Butler as Epifania Ognisanti di Pareria, Paul Craig as Alastair Fitzfassenden, Mary Barton as Patricia Smith

Then came the tumultuous year of Barry Morse as artistic director of the Shaw Festival. With his inexhaustible energy and his unceasing flow of imaginative ideas—he is the total man of the theatre—he transformed the Festival forever in one season.

Working with Barry was like going over Niagara Falls in a barrel. In the early part of the season, when Barry was still filming his television series, *The Fugitive,* he was a man in constant motion. I remember one occasion when Ray Wickens and I drove him from Niagara-on-the-Lake to Toronto to catch a plane. During the drive he overwhelmed us with a long list of suggestions about publicity, ticket sales, staff, remodelling and redecorating the theatre—a hundred details about a dozen matters. He was still shouting last-minute brain waves as he rushed to board the plane. We drove back to Niagara-on-the-Lake bemused. I'd hardly had a chance to settle down at home when the telephone rang. It was Barry. He had just landed in California and must communicate to me at once a new flood of ideas and suggestions.

First Barry extended the season to nine weeks and then he chose a spectacular and challenging group of plays: *Man and Superman, Misalliance,* and *The Apple Cart.* He launched a whirlwind casting campaign with dozens of telephone calls and personal interviews. In the end he recruited a fine company of actors, which included Zoe Caldwell, Susan Clark, Pat Galloway, Tom Kneebone, Henry Ramer, Leslie Yeo, Sandy Webster, Patrick Boxill, Hugh Webster, and the man who was to be so important to our future, Paxton Whitehead. But best of all Barry generated a spirit among the Festival workers of great expectations and great accomplishments.

The season was a triumph. Audiences increased to ninety-eight per cent of capacity. The critics' notices were very favourable, and now the Festival had gained the attention of newspapers across Canada and in many parts of the United States as well. We received our first grant from the Canada Council in the amount of $2,400. In a mood of great optimism, the

Festival Board at its annual meeting in November of 1966 established a study committee for a new theatre. Now the search was on in earnest.

Barry couldn't stay with us beyond that one season, but I still remember his parting shot. Why not a geodesic dome to house our theatre? A geodesic dome in historic Niagara-on-the-Lake!

The exciting mood of that year is perhaps best conveyed by Barry himself as he reminisced about it a few years later.

A SEASON TO REMEMBER

It's a blustery day toward the end of 1965, and I'm sitting in the University Club in Toronto. Across the table from me sits Brian Doherty—beaming with bonhomie and bubbling with news of the Shaw Festival. Would I like to have a bash with them next year? I blink and think. At this time, my life is mostly taken up with the pursuit of some chap in a Hollywood-telly-series, so I must confer with my producer and my agents.

Back in California I confront my amiable boss Quinn Martin. Full of wild surmise, I tell him what I'd like to do, and he—good workmate that he is—indulgently agrees (in the manner of one dealing with an old friend stricken with some unaccountable malaise) to give me at least the three months that I think necessary to get the season launched. Then back to Toronto and Brian. The venture has already infected me with a desperado daring and I suggest that we make our season longer than ever before (nine whole weeks!) and that we do three plays, the first of them one of the largest, longest, and most complex in the whole Shaw canon: *Man and Superman* (and at something like full length). Then *Misalliance*—then *The Apple Cart*.

So the plays are picked; the dates are set; and now the images begin to blur. I meet a scrubbed, blue-eyed choirboy named Raymond Wickens, who they tell me is our Business Manager, Publicity Director, and

Lord-High-Everything-Else and he takes me down to Niagara-on-the-Lake. (Shame on me! I've never set foot in the place before.) We view our theatre—the Court House. Its interior, our womb of mysteries, is painted an acidulated public-urinal green and looks bleakly unpromising. No time for dismay to settle—maybe we can do something about that later. The plays have to be cast.

There now begins an exciting round of cajolery, blandishment, arm-twisting, foot-licking, exploiting of old friends, inflammation of total strangers, and the outlay of almost everything except money. The fever is catching: all manner of theatre workers, some eminent, some novices, are willing to throw in their lots with us under working conditions and for rewards which, in most cases, are infinitely lower than they could reasonably expect in their normal working lives. This is the grandest kind of largesse; these are the richest subsidies any theatre venture could ever have.

Their names are a luscious litany to remember—Zoe Caldwell, Pat Galloway, Betty Leighton, Susan Clark, Tom Kneebone, Leslie Yeo, Hugh Webster, Norman Welsh, and a young man of sonorous voice and twinkling-solemn manner named Paxton Whitehead—and many, many more—fine troupers all!

Whilst we're assembling our troupe, we're pressing on with two other projects which become known among us as 'warming up the town' and 'beating the drum'. The citizenry of Niagara-on-the-Lake is not unqualified or unanimous in its enthusiasm for the Shaw Festival. There are obviously those (there may still be) who hope that we may quietly go away or, better still, that a righteous Providence may visit fire and brimstone upon us and all our sinful pleasurable works. We encounter bloody-mindedness as well as saintly kindliness, but quite perceptibly the town warms up.

We beat the drum in every way we can (short of spending money). A wider world is beginning to hear of the Shaw Festival. Raymond brings us word whilst we wrestle with rehearsals in Toronto that we're actually selling large numbers of seats.

We move down to Niagara and into the Court House (still public urinal green). We build the stage and elevate the seating. We arrange to have a monstrous rocket fired from the roof of the building by the local military at the moment of the beginning of the first performance.

Dress rehearsals—and a preview.

The eleventh hour—close to the starting line.

And now, late at night on the eve of our opening, our Stage Manager, Larry Wayne appears with gallons of paint and dozens of rollers and brushes and we set about painting the auditorium a friendlier shade. All of us. All those pampered show-biz layabouts are up ladders with babushkas round their heads painting for dear life. We're still putting on the finishing dabs when Raymond appears, dinner-jacketed, to tell us that our first night audience is at the doors. We scamper to the kitchen which is our only dressing room (the sexes are loosely divided by a sagging curtain) to get our slap on. Five minutes. Hundreds of wires from well-wishers. Pinned to the call-board with a stage nail is a message apparently from Queen Elizabeth I: 'By your courage in the field and your conduct in the camp, we shall shortly have a Famous Victory.'

'Overture and Beginners please!'

Scrambling back from the front of the house, where I've been to ensure that all our first night Worthies are properly ensconced, I bump into Paxton, palely loitering, ready for Octavius. We hug each other convulsively and he soundlessly mouths one word: 'Relax!' I try.

A shuddering thud and decrescendo roar. Our rocket on the roof is off, and so are we. . . .

Our second night, and in the dark of the wings Leslie Yeo gives me a jubilant 'thumbs up'. We're sold out!

And so we were all season long.

*Tom Kneebone as Henry Straker, Barry
Morse as John Tanner*

*Norman Welsh as the Statue, Hugh
Webster as the Devil, Pat Galloway as
Doña Ana, Barry Morse as Don Juan in* ▷
the 'Hell Scene'

MISALLIANCE

. . . The aviator's crashing companion is Lina, Polish acrobat, characterized by Miss Zoe Caldwell with perfectly marvelous hypnotic eyes and staggering physical prowess which allows her to overcome obstreperous males and carry them around like venison. . . .
Ardis Smith, *Buffalo Evening News*

Zoe Caldwell as Lina Szczepanowska, Tom Kneebone as Bentley Summerhays

Susan Clark as Hypatia Tarleton, Paul Craig as Johnny Tarleton, Betty Leighton as Mrs Tarleton, Tom Kneebone as Bentley Summerhays ▷

. . . Howard Lever is altogether marvellous as the little man who crashes in waving a pistol, hides in the steam bath, threatens all sorts of people and in the end is taken under Mrs. Tarleton's wing. He brings out the deep feeling of frustration in the little man, at the same time producing the most hilarious moments in the play. . . .

E. H. Lampard
The St Catharines Standard

Howard Lever as 'Gunner', Leslie Yeo as John Tarleton

Michael Bradshaw as Joseph Percival, Susan Clark as Hypatia Tarleton

. . . As only the best string players can interpret a Beethoven quartet, none but the best, or at least superlatively good actors should attempt the Shavian composition. Last night's Shavians [in *Misalliance*], under the direction of Barry Morse, were at least superlatively good. . . .

Ralph Hicklin
The Globe and Mail, Toronto

Michael Bradshaw as Joseph Percival, Tom Kneebone as Bentley Summerhays, Zoe Caldwell as Lina Szczepanowska, Leslie Yeo as John Tarleton, Betty Leighton as Mrs Tarleton

. . . Mr. Whitehead is the ideal Shavian. As King Magnus, Shaw's imaginary monarch of the future, he is asked to deliver lengthy speeches about the complexities of politics that in lesser hands could become pedantic. However, he possesses both a sharpness of mind that makes the complexities clear, and a passion for the true wonder of the world that is warmly contagious. . . .

As the king's mistress, Orinthia, Miss Caldwell fashions a superb comic portrait of female vanity. She is triumphant as she sneers at another woman for being so bourgeois as to "trot through the streets *shopping*." She is glorious as she exults, "Thank God my self-consciousness is something nobler than vulgar conceit in having *done* something." And she tops it all regally in a rowdily passionate forgetting of her elegance to wrestle the king to the floor of her boudoir. . . .

Henry Hewes, *Saturday Review*

Zoe Caldwell as Orinthia, Paxton Whitehead as King Magnus

Howard Lever as Sempronius, Michael
Bradshaw as Pamphilius, Alfred Gallagher
as Crassus, Sandy Webster as Pliny, Jon
Granik as Balbus, Sheila Haney as
Amanda, Margaret MacLeod as Lysistrata

Foreground: Henry Ramer as Boanerges,
Patrick Boxill as Proteus, Betty Leighton
as Queen Jemima

The years from 1967 to 1971 were years of counterpoint with two themes constantly intertwining: the growing success and recognition of the stage productions and the continuing search for a site for a permanent theatre.

Paxton Whitehead, who succeeded Barry Morse as artistic director in 1967, was the principal orchestrator of the first theme. He set out to prove himself and prove himself he did. Like Andrew Allan and Barry Morse before him, he was a complete, skilled, intelligent professional, highly aware of the practical aspects of the theatre. At the same time he had a very personal talent which he demonstrated in the unique way in which he managed to combine safety and daring.

Paxton continued to extend the Festival season: to ten weeks in 1969, to eleven weeks in 1970, and to twelve weeks in 1971. And he showed sound judgement in his choice of programs. Certainly the audiences that crowded into the Court House Theatre registered consistent delight. Indeed in 1968 the company played to an astounding 101 per cent of capacity. So popular were the plays that year that extra seats had to be brought in at almost every performance to accommodate the overflow. And the critics seemed largely to agree with the audience. Dan Sullivan of *The New York Times* likened the production of *Heartbreak House* in the Court House to 'finding a Watteau at a country auction'. Caedmon Records admired the production, too, enough to record it in its entirety.

Through these years Paxton Whitehead attracted a procession of gifted actors to the Festival, some of them world renowned. In 1967 Kate Reid appeared as Lady Catherine Champion-Cheney in Somerset Maugham's *The Circle*. In 1968 Jessica Tandy came to Niagara-on-the-Lake to play Hesione Hushabye in *Heartbreak House*. In 1969 Lila Kedrova played in Ferenc Molnár's *The Guardsman*. In 1970 Stanley Holloway played Burgess in *Candida*. He was to return to play the Waiter in *You Never Can Tell* in the inaugural season in the new theatre.

All the while Paxton continued to win acclaim as an actor. In 1967 he gave us a hugely comic Sergius in *Arms and the Man* and in 1971 a virtuoso rollick in the title role in *The Philanderer.* While he directed some of the plays, he also brought in a number of talented guest directors: Edward Gilbert for *Arms and the Man* and *Major Barbara* in 1967; Val Gielgud, best known for his masterly work at the BBC in England, for the triumphant *Heartbreak House* of 1968; Stephen Porter for *The Guardsman* and Dillon Evans for *The Doctor's Dilemma* in 1969; the American actor-director Harris Yulin for *Candida* in 1970; and Tony van Bridge for *The Philanderer* in 1971.

Along with others, Paxton played his part in encouraging innovation at the Festival. In 1967 the company went on tour for the first time. At the end of the season at Niagara-on-the-Lake, they took *Major Barbara* to the Port Royal Theatre at Expo 67 in Montreal and then on to the Manitoba Theatre Centre in Winnipeg. Two years later we made our début at the National Arts Centre in Ottawa, with the 1969 production of *The Guardsman.* In 1970 there was a pre-season tour of *Candida* to Kingston and Ottawa. And in the spring of the following year came the most ambitious tour to date: *The Philanderer* was presented in Kingston, Montreal, Ottawa, and Rochester, New York, where the company played for the first time in the United States.

Music came to the Shaw Festival and the Court House stage in 1969 with *Five Variations for Corno di Bassetto,* an interesting entertainment written by Louis Applebaum and Ronald Hambleton. John Horton played Shaw the music critic. Then in 1970 and 1971 the Orford Quartet and the Lyric Trio (billed as *Music Today*) gave a few concerts of contemporary music in St Mark's Anglican Church. The programs drew considerable critical praise.

In these years we continued to present occasional plays by writers other than Shaw. Paxton Whitehead and Suzanne Grossmann made an English translation of Georges Feydeau's *La Main Passe,* which they entitled *The Chemmy Circle.* It had its world première at the 1968 Festival and it was a hit. That same year Micheál MacLiammóir was invited to bring his celebrated one-man show, *The Importance of Being Oscar,* to the Festival. In 1970 Tony van Bridge compiled and performed *G.K.C.,* a presentation based on the writings of Shaw's contemporary G. K. Chesterton. Even the avant-garde found its place at the Festival in 1971 with *Summer Days,* Suzanne Grossmann's translation of a French fantasy, *L'Été,* by Romain Weingarten.

There were many new faces at the Shaw Festival in these years. In 1967 Maurice Strike, a gifted set designer, joined the company. He created many highly original and imaginative sets, beginning with an exquisite golden-yellow drawing room for *The Circle.* That same year Hilary Corbett, who like Maurice is still with us, arrived to design and produce costumes to complement the imaginative sets.

And there were new faces in the business office as well. We had come a long way from those early years when the grind of administration depended on unpaid volunteers. Now we had a professional staff. At the end of 1967 Muriel Sherrin came to the Festival as its first general manager, and she brought to the job extraordinary energy, tenacity, and leadership. It was no coincidence that in 1969 the Festival broke all previous box office records, with a total sale of $120,872. Muriel had an instinct for recruiting the right people to work with her. During her tenure she brought in Judith Hendry as publicity director, Nancy Strike as Judith's assistant, and Beverley Mitchell as business manager.

Muriel retired from the Festival in 1971 and was succeeded in June of that year by Thomas Burrows. Nothing seemed to daunt or discourage Tom, and his energy and ability were to serve us well. In addition to his other duties, he assumed the responsibility for guiding the Festival toward its new theatre.

Now more than ever the need for a new theatre was on everyone's mind. All sorts of ideas were considered and abandoned. At the directors' meeting in June of 1967 the idea of buying some of the Expo buildings and removing them to Niagara-on-the-Lake was discussed. There was a tentative plan that the Toronto Symphony Orchestra might co-operate in this effort and establish a summer base at Niagara-on-the-Lake.

By 1968 it was clear that the only satisfactory answer was a new building. In December of that year Douglas Buck was appointed development co-ordinator. For several years he and many other members of the Festival Board and staff viewed and assessed almost every piece of vacant land (of a suitable size) in Niagara-on-the-Lake and the surrounding countryside. For me the search became almost an obsession. I couldn't go for a walk or a drive without pondering the suitability of the places I passed.

For a short time the Queen's Royal Park on Lake Ontario at the foot of King Street looked promising, but the land belonged to the town and in the end the council would not agree to sell it. Similarly, for a time in 1969 the old military common opposite Fort George appeared to be the answer to our search. The land was owned by the federal government, which decided to offer us instead a site at the opposite end of town on the local golf course beside Fort Mississauga and overlooking the lake.

As soon as word of that proposal spread through town, a small but vocal group of residents launched a campaign of opposition. Owners of houses bordering on the golf course led the attack, which became a very real one when one member of the group threatened me with an upraised putter one day on the golf course. Most of the opposition, however, was registered through letters to local papers and speeches to the local council. The federal government withdrew its offer, and the Festival returned to its unrewarding search.

The search was not, of course, proceeding in a vacuum. While some of us combed the area for a suitable site, others were exploring new ideas in theatre design. And still others were hard at work raising money to pay for the construction of a new theatre. How much money would we need to see it through to completion? Not less than $2.6 million we decided.

From its early years the Festival had conducted a very productive fund-raising operation, which now had the continuing support of many private contributors as well as the Ontario Arts Council and the Canada Council. At the beginning of 1970 the building-fund drive, under the general direction of Calvin Rand, shifted to a new level of intensity. Influential new directors from Toronto, London, and Hamilton joined the Festival Board. Committees organized fund-raising functions in the Niagara peninsula, in Hamilton, in Buffalo, and in Toronto. The results in Toronto warranted our renting a small office there to co-ordinate financial activities in the Metro area.

Bit by bit we began to accumulate a respectable building fund, which was increased substantially by the grants the directors were able to negotiate with the federal government and the government of Ontario. The latter approved a grant of $500,000 in May of 1970, and the federal government matched that amount in September of 1971. Now the Festival coffers boasted a grand total of $1.7 million.

Some of the money went for a design for the new theatre. More than twenty architects were considered before we chose Ron Thom, a Toronto architect who had begun his career in Vancouver. He was an ideal choice, a man of accomplishment in his own field and of great sympathy for the theatre.

By now it appeared that we had a site. It was known as Market Square and lay directly behind the Court House. Market Square offered a few problems, the principal one being that it was smaller than we might have wished. But it was centrally located. The town of Niagara-on-the-Lake owned the land, and on June 25, 1970, the town council voted to lease it to the Festival for a long period. It seemed that the trying search for a theatre site had at last come to an end.

That happy illusion didn't last long. Almost immediately there were problems—problems involving general services, parking facilities, zoning, the closing of right-of-ways. There were objections from some of the townspeople, from a group that championed the preservation of old Ontario architecture, and even from some local politicians. Very little of this resistance had been evident during the weeks of negotiation between the Festival and the town, but with the signing of the lease—and Ron Thom hard at work on plans and drawings—objections and difficulties multiplied. The obstacles proved overwhelming, and in December of 1971 the Festival agreed to abandon its claim to the Market Square site.

And yet that stormy and discouraging month of December was to end on a happy note. When we began to realize in the fall of 1971 that the opposition to the Market Square site would be insurmountable, we approached the Department of Indian Affairs and Northern Development about another site. By the end of the year, it was ours.

The resolution emerged from a complex, exhausting, but mercifully brief series of negotiations that involved the Festival with the Department of Indian Affairs and Northern Development, the Niagara Hospital, the Niagara-on-the-Lake Town Council, the Boy Scout Committee, the Niagara-on-the-Lake Golf Club, and many concerned local residents. All had claims on the site in question, but all very graciously surrendered those claims. And what of the new site? It was ideal—only two blocks along the main street from the Court House —an old military camp ground that fronted on Wellington Street.

While the battles over sites raged through 1970 and 1971, Ron Thom had been studying Niagara-on-the-Lake, its architecture and its special atmosphere. He conferred regularly with Festival committees and staff and with technical advisers as he applied himself to the challenge of creating a new theatre. By the end of 1971 he had a plan.

Ron has written of the obstacles he faced in his assignment: 'A theatre is as complex and even dangerous a design problem as an architect is likely to meet. In part the theatre is an intricate piece of machinery. Various elements can be calculated in precise quantitative terms—how high is a fly gallery, how steep is the auditorium rake and so on—many of them complicated but still *concrete* problems, capable of precise solution.

'At the centre, however, is a mystery—*the actor and his audience*—the event which the whole complex machine is set in motion to support. It is the crucial relationship between these two, a fragile, intangible conjunction, that is the soul of the theatre.'

Ron went on to acknowledge the help of the Festival and its people in his research: 'They knew what kind of theatre they wanted and how it had to operate. Their instructions were clear, their research thorough.'

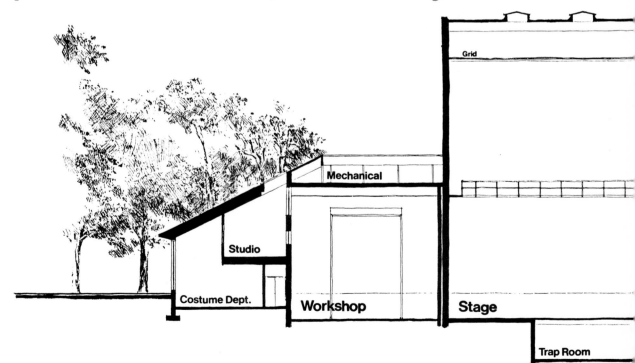

Ron's design seemed to realize and encompass all our dreams. The building, a contemporary structure, used natural materials, wood shingles and brick. The auditorium, which would seat just over eight hundred people, was wood panelled, with a proscenium-arch stage. The backstage area was roomy enough to accommodate administrative, rehearsal, and workshop facilities, and to permit all members of the company to work under the same roof. In sum, the conception was beautiful and practical, with a very distinctive look, but a look that was entirely compatible with the ambience of Niagara-on-the-Lake.

That first design had to be altered, since it was intended for the Market Square site. Late in 1971 Ron set about revamping the plans. As the year ended, the mood for 1972 was confident. Bring on the new challenge—the construction of the theatre.

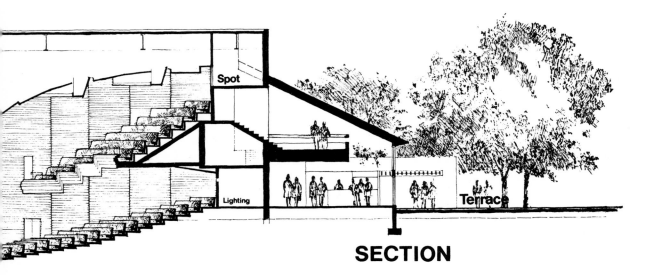

SECTION

1 9 6 7

ARMS AND THE MAN

Martha Henry as Raina Petkoff

Sandy Webster as Major Petkoff, Martha Henry as Raina Petkoff, Paxton Whitehead as Sergius, Douglas Rain as Captain Bluntschli

63

Betty Leighton as Catherine Petkoff, Sandy Webster as Major Petkoff

. . . Douglas Rain's Swiss is a beautifully precise, economic character; falling-down exhausted but still impeccably polite when he's on the run, blunt, assured, level-headed in his steel-rim spectacles when he returns as the gracious lover.

Paxton Whitehead's cavalry dandy, by contrast, starts out all courtly and correct, fluting and faultless, but winds up snivelling and clutching at any skirt that whisks by in the end.

Martha Henry as Raina Petkoff, Douglas Rain as Captain Bluntschli

Martha Henry's portrayal of Raina is a vocal tour de force. When she's playing the high-born, illusion-ridden lady (and this is truly a role within a role) her voice is like a limousine horn, imperious, commanding. When she's brought down to her true level with a thump by the plain-speaking Swiss, it becomes all feminine and lilting. And she switches easily back and forth between the two, perfectly delineating Raina's mercuric switches of temperament.

Paxton Whitehead as Sergius, Suzanne Grossmann as Louka

Heath Lamberts as Nicola, Suzanne Grossmann as Louka

Suzanne Grossmann plays Louka, the defiant maid who swears she'll never have the "soul of a servant," with an unforced but vivacious naturalness and makes the girl a curious, grating delight. Her scenes with the panting Paxton Whitehead are among the best of the evening. Heath Lamberts as an obsequious butler, who's always aware of exactly which side his bread is butled on, displays a stunning mastery of timing for one so young. . . .

Ron Evans, *The Telegram*, Toronto

Susan Ringwood as Elizabeth, Paul Collins as Edward Luton

THE CIRCLE
W. Somerset Maugham

Kate Reid as Lady Catherine Champion-Cheney, Hiram Sherman as Clive Champion-Cheney
Background: Paul Collins as Edward Luton, Susan Ringwood as Elizabeth, Steven Sutherland as Arnold Champion-Cheney

67

*Kate Reid as Lady Catherine
Champion-Cheney, Leslie Yeo as Lord
Porteous, Hiram Sherman as Clive
Champion-Cheney*

MAJOR BARBARA

Roy Cooper as Bill Walker, Patrick Boxill as Peter Shirley, Irena Mayeska as Barbara Undershaft

69

*Eric House as Snobby Price, Jennifer
Phipps as Rummy Mitchens*

*Paxton Whitehead as Adolphus Cusins,
Irena Mayeska as Barbara Undershaft*

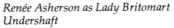

Larry Gates as Andrew Undershaft, Renée Asherson as Lady Britomart Undershaft

Renée Asherson as Lady Britomart Undershaft

Having completed a highly-successful debut as the final play of the season at Niagara-on-the-Lake's annual Shaw Festival, Edward Gilbert's production of Bernard Shaw's "Major Barbara" gave the first of eight performances for Expo's World Festival at the Place des Arts' Port Royal Theatre Saturday evening before moving to Winnipeg to become the first presentation of the season at the Manitoba Theatre Centre, where Mr. Gilbert is artistic director.

The capacity audience, which went on applauding long after the cast stopped taking curtain calls, must have left the theatre stimulated by two principal reactions—the clarity and smoothness of Mr. Gilbert's production and the amazing topicality of Shaw's text. . . .

Sydney Johnson, *The Montreal Star*

71

Larry Gates as Andrew Undershaft,
Paxton Whitehead as Adolphus Cusins,
Margaret MacLeod as Mrs Baines,
Deborah Kipp as Jenny Hill, Roy Cooper as
Bill Walker

. . . To come across a really elegant production of "Heartbreak House" in this setting is a little like finding a Watteau at a country auction. Or would be, if you hadn't heard so many good things in advance about Niagara's Shaw Festival. . . .

At any rate, one flight above Niagara's one-cell jail this summer you may see a "Heartbreak House" that would be worth going to London to see. The production's Boss Mangan, Bill Fraser, is, in fact, fresh from the London production with Irene Worth, and he couldn't have been more impressive there than he is here.

"Heartbreak House," one of Shaw's most difficult plays, is his metaphor for England just before World War I: a house fatally divided between neurotics and bullies.

One of the paradoxes of the situation is that the bullies are, underneath, as soft as the neurotics. Mr. Fraser's performance brings this out marvelously, his face melting from the toughness of an Otto Preminger to the mildness of a Robert Benchley as the pressure increases.

Tony van Bridge as Captain Shotover, Jessica Tandy as Hesione Hushabye, Paxton Whitehead as Hector Hushabye

73

Applying the pressure with equal facility and elegance are Jessica Tandy's Hesione Hushabye, a lady who would probably be amused by the Second Coming, and Frances Hyland's Lady Utterword, who has just arrived from what Shaw calls "Horseback Hall" and cannot wait to get back there. You start by laughing at Miss Hyland's rhinestone manners; you end up in awe of the hard rock beneath them.

Mr. van Bridge's Captain Shotover is a memorable combination of doddering senility and patriarchal sense, and Mr. Whitehead's Hector Hushabye, the neurotic who just might grow up in time, is a comic sketch that very soon becomes a man.

Val Gielgud's direction is crisp, without stinting on the marvelously haunted feeling of the last scene, when the gods of war ride over "Heartbreak House" in their new chariots. Maurice Strike's setting does wonders in the tiny space assigned. . . .

Dan Sullivan, *The New York Times*

Bill Fraser as Boss Mangan, Jessica Tandy as Hesione Hushabye

Eleanor Beecroft as Nurse Guinness,
Frances Hyland as Lady Utterword, James
Valentine as Randall Utterword

Patrick Boxill as Mazzini Dunn, Diana LeBlanc as Ellie Dunn, Tony van Bridge as Captain Shotover, James Valentine as Randall Utterword, Frances Hyland as Lady Utterword, Bill Fraser as Boss Mangan, Jessica Tandy as Hesione Hushabye, Paxton Whitehead as Hector Hushabye

THE IMPORTANCE OF BEING OSCAR
Excerpts from Oscar Wilde's works

Micheál MacLiammóir

THE CHEMMY CIRCLE

World première *The Chemmy Circle* adapted by Suzanne Grossmann
From Georges Feydeau's *La Main Passe*

All the ingredients of fun, violence, and ribaldry are present and generally well accounted for in The Chemmy Circle, the play by Georges Feydeau which opened last night at the Court House Theatre. Even though there are times when the farce speedometer decelerates more than is wise for it, this final attraction of the 1968 Shaw festival reaches a high index of amusement.

Give artistic director Paxton Whitehead the major credit for making the English language premiere of the Feydeau play an event of good cheer. Working with Suzanne Grossmann's translation, he has staged the action with an acute understanding of its components.

The emphasis is on comic dash and zestfulness, best embodied by the leading performances of Frances Hyland, John Horton, Jack Creley, Patricia Gage and James Valentine and further buttressed by sturdy cameos by Kenneth Dight, James Cull, Kenneth Wickes and Whitehead himself as a French parliamentarian who, a model of poise and oratory the rest of the time, stutters and stumbles when he is in the throes of undeclared desire. . . .

Nathan Cohen, *The Toronto Star*

Patricia Gage as Sophie Fédot, James Cull as LaPige, Kenneth Dight as Belgence, Patrick Boxill as Planteloup

Jack Creley as Hubertin, James Valentine as Fédot, Frances Hyland as Francine Chanal

Paxton Whitehead as Coustouillu, John Horton as Chanal, Frances Hyland as Francine Chanal

James Valentine as Fédot, John Horton as Chanal

*Sam Moses as Leo Schutzmacher, Robert
Flemyng as Sir Colenso Ridgeon*

81

*Helen Finn as Jennifer Dubedat, Paxton
Whitehead as Louis Dubedat*

Helen Finn as Jennifer Dubedat, Malcolm Armstrong as the Young Man

Robert Flemyng as Sir Colenso Ridgeon, James Edmond as Sir Patrick Cullen

Robert Flemyng as Sir Colenso Ridgeon,
Patrick Boxill as Blenkinsop, Kenneth
Dight as Cutler Walpole, David
Hutcheson as Sir Ralph Bloomfield
Bonington

Frances Hyland as Eve

FIVE VARIATIONS FOR CORNO DI BASSETTO

Patrick Boxill as Compère

Standing: John Horton as Corno di Bassetto

Seated beside pianist: Patrick Boxill as Compère

Musicians: Gerard Kantarjian (violin), Jay Morton (clarinet), Reginald Godden (piano), Albin Berky (cello), Mary Simmons (soprano)

THE GUARDSMAN
Ferenc Molnár
English version by Frank Marcus

George Bernard, patron saint of the
Shaw Festival, himself admired Ferenc
Molnar's comedy, The Guardsman,
quite extravagantly. Short of speech and
brittle as was Shaw long-winded, it
makes a very welcome addition to the
season here, crowning it, in fact. . . .

Madame Kedrova presents the role as
a famous soubrette of the Budapest
stage, for all the reference to her Dame
aux Camellias. She is like a delicious pet
Pekingese, full of charming moues, little
gestures and great, embracing smiles.

She frisks around Maurice Strike's
gorgeous drawing room setting with the
gaiety of a great entertainer on an
important cabaret opening. . . .

So far, Madame Kedrova has been
setting up the situation and the woman
in it. In the last act, she gets down to
work. Suddenly extending her range,
she enters into the husband's
interrogation with fire. She beats him
into submission, then when he discloses
his impersonation, beats him into
submission again. At last she relaxes;

Lila Kedrova as the Actress, Ilona; Paxton
Whitehead as the Actor, Nandor

87

she has enjoyed her double triumph and is satisfied—at least for the moment. But it is still spring. . . .

The Whitehead role is heaven-sent, for it is twofold. He is beautifully the insanely jealous Actor, devoured by his suspicions. Then he switches to the Guardsman, overlaying the one role on another.

His Guardsman is almost a general, stiff and pompous, where his Actor had been sleek and nervy. . . .

Hanna Sarvasova bustles through the role of the Mama with great spirit, while Carl Don gives the Critic-Confidant the sophistication of a variety star. Susan King is a wholly delightful aid and Tibor Feheregyhazi plays his two scenes as the Creditor impeccably, summoning a whole world of Budapest theatre in a few words. . . .

Herbert Whittaker
The Globe and Mail, Toronto

Lila Kedrova as the Actress, Ilona; Paxton Whitehead as the Actor, Nandor

*Tibor Feheregyhazi as the Creditor,
Rosenzweig*

*Margot Sweeney as the Cook, Susan King
as the Maid, Liesl*

Hanna Sarvasova as the 'Mother'

. . . Miss Hyland, in my opinion, could play any role from Minnie the Moocher to Mother Macree, and she brings a complete understanding to Shaw's study of the essential female. She is handsome, charming, intelligent, agreeable, courageous and practical, obviously an excellent housekeeper, a devoted wife and a model mother.

She is also acquisitive, tenacious and selfish, with a will of iron and an instinctive drive to manage others. Miss Hyland portrays very subtly this formidable female instinct. . . .

The manly man in the case is Candida's husband, the Reverend James Morell, played by Tony van Bridge. . . . He is strong, imposing, kind, frank, sincere, genial, tolerant, upright, concerned for the welfare of others, and unselfish in giving his own

Tony van Bridge as Morell, Stanley Holloway as Burgess, Frances Hyland as Candida

talents and energies to the causes he believes in.

Mr. van Bridge shows us all this, but he also shows us what Shaw undoubtedly wanted us to see: . . . he is somewhat pompous, harmlessly vain in his self-assured moral attitudes and his belief in his ability to deal with people. . . .

Burgess, Candida's father, is played by Stanley Holloway. At 80 Mr. Holloway gambols through his part with an astonishing verve and sprightliness. Mr. Holloway, of course, knows exactly how and when to be funny, and he treats the role of Burgess as a proper vehicle for his talents, making that unregenerate opportunist and exploiter of labour a sympathetic character. . . .

Berners W. Jackson, *Professor of English*
McMaster University
The Spectator, Hamilton

Leslie Carlson as Lexy, Jennifer Phipps as Prossy

Stanley Holloway as Burgess, Frances Hyland as Candida, Chris Sarandon as Marchbanks

Chris Sarandon as Marchbanks, Frances Hyland as Candida

G.K.C.
The Wit and Wisdom of Gilbert Keith Chesterton

. . . Tony van Bridge, that admirable performer of Shakespeare, Shaw and Brecht, made his entrance in the character of G.K.C. . . . Cane-carrying and cloaked, with his hair done in the manner recorded by Hilaire Belloc and Max Beerbohm . . .

Mr. van Bridge is careful not to claim an impersonation, but he certainly does suggest a likeness. He has a way of falling into silence that is most impressive. He has the gleam of high intelligence. He is certainly benign. And he wins immediate sympathy by recounting his rude rebuff to a rude remark by Bernard Shaw about the G.K.C. girth. . . .

For the second half of the program the actor abandoned the bulky creator in favor of his tiny creation, Father Brown. He told the first of Chesterton's Father Brown detective stories, The Blue Cross, and made every character in it come alive for us. It is a truly festive event when a performer, in one evening, can so happily revive both the art of impersonation and the art of storytelling. . . .

Herbert Whittaker
The Globe and Mail, Toronto

Tony van Bridge as G.K.C.

FORTY YEARS ON
Alan Bennett

*Christopher Szczucinski as one of the boys
of Albion House, Robert Harris as the
Headmaster*

Robert Harris as Headmaster, with two of
the boys of Albion House

Jennifer Phipps as Matron, with one of the
boys of Albion House

The boys of Albion House

*Paxton Whitehead as Tempest, Amelia
Hall as Miss Nisbitt*

*Paxton Whitehead as Tempest, Alan Scarfe
as Franklin*

. . . This production's glory is a really grand performance—Paxton Whitehead as Charteris. Silly, infuriating, but always recognizable, this is a man given to sweet, idiotic grins at just those moments when others are abusing his reputation.

Shrinking hideously from the truth ("It hurts"), jack-knifing his way across the stage in a split second, betrayed constantly by a face that won't obey orders, Whitehead contributes a major piece of acting. . . .

He is assisted by two very spectacular-looking women. Patricia Collins' Grace is absolutely splendid, as rigid as if she had been memorialized in bronze.

By contrast, Louise Marleau's Julia is all quivering, ingenuous femininity, but with real accents of the Ibsenite passion. . . .

The Philanderer is given the kind of stylishly Edwardian production that has come to be the Shaw Festival's hallmark. . . . But all the external trappings are really only a platform for words, and given Paxton Whitehead and his very merry company, the words take off and soar.

The Toronto Star

Louise Marleau as Julia Craven, Paxton Whitehead as Leonard Charteris

*Standing: Paxton Whitehead as Leonard
Charteris, Norman Welsh as Joseph
Cuthbertson, Diana Barrington as Sylvia
Craven, Patrick Boxill as Colonel Craven*

*Foreground: Louise Marleau as Julia
Craven, Patricia Collins as Grace
Tranfield, James Valentine as Dr Paramore*

SUMMER DAYS
Romain Weingarten
Translated by Suzanne Grossmann

Derek McGrath as Simon, Nancy Beatty as Lorette

Shadow Play

Paxton Whitehead as Simon Gayforth,
Carole Shelley as Victoria Gayforth,
Barbara Hamilton as Martha Cunningham

Family Album

. . . Patrick Boxill, making his only appearance of the evening [in *Family Album*], walked off with everybody's heart as the ancient servitor who has the last word. . . .

Herbert Whittaker
The Globe and Mail, Toronto

Standing: Hiram Sherman as Jasper Featherways, Derek McGrath as Richard Featherways, Michael Hogan as Charles Winter, Paxton Whitehead as Edward Valance, Patrick Boxill as Burrows
Seated: Barbara Hamilton as Lavinia Featherways, Carole Shelley as Jane Featherways, Nancy Beatty as Harriet Winter, Susan Hogan as Emily Valance

A Social Success
Max Beerbohm

*James Valentine as Tommy Dixon, Susan
Hogan as the Countess of Amersham*

O'Flaherty, V.C.

Michael Hogan as O'Flaherty, Barbara Hamilton as Mrs O'Flaherty, Patrick Boxill as Sir Pearce, Susan Hogan as Teresa

Michael Hogan as O'Flaherty, Susan Hogan as Teresa

Press Cuttings

Carole Shelley as Lady Corinthia, James Valentine as General Mitchener

Barbara Hamilton as Mrs Banger

Patrick Boxill as Balsquith

James Valentine as General Mitchener,
Eric House as the Orderly

Despite the bright atmosphere of go-ahead, there were still kinks to be smoothed out. Through the early months of 1972, Festival Board officers Dr Donald MacDonald, Leo Sauve, and Henry Wiens along with Tom Burrows and his staff worked at implementing the agreements that the Festival had put together in such a flurry in the final weeks of 1971. Some matters were serious enough—the necessary approval of the Ontario Municipal Board for the Niagara-on-the-Lake by-law to permit rezoning of the new site as a theatre. But some of the details that cropped up afforded us a few chuckles: Tom found that we had to provide insurance for any golfer who might be unlucky enough to strike a Festival patron with a wild shot.

In the meantime Ron Thom had reworked the design to fit the new site. His final plan maintained the distinctive grace of the earlier one, the same contemporary feeling. It made use of the same natural materials, and happily it complied with the requirements of the Niagara Planning Board and the town council. One of those requirements was that the height of the theatre should not exceed the eighty feet of the cherished maples that lined Wellington Street. The plan provided parking space, but best of all it made

Brian Doherty turning the first sod at the site of the new Shaw Festival Theatre on April 17, 1972

eye-catching use of the extra land. There was a reflecting pool, and there were landscaped terraces laid out to provide a green prospect from any point inside the theatre's garden lobby.

With a great sense of wonder, joy, and gratitude on April 17, 1972, I turned the first sod at the new site. Our permanent theatre was under way. After the seemingly interminable struggle to find the right site, the building itself moved quickly. Ron Thom was to write later of 'the personal commitment and dedication of the builders of the building—from the carpenters to the weavers of the curtain. They have done their work with great care and skill.' Frequently as I visited the site while construction was under way, I, too, was struck with the same appreciation of the obvious zeal of all the workers.

'Why?' I asked the foreman of the project one day. 'Why are these men so dedicated to their work?'

'It's a challenge,' he told me. 'They've never worked on a theatre before and probably never will again. They really care about getting it right.'

Still, the generous spirit that pervaded the construction of the theatre required tangible support. At the end of 1971 we needed at least another million dollars to complete the project—right down to the last piece of

Calvin Rand receiving the Government of Canada's cheque for $500,000 from the Hon.J. J. Greene at the ground breaking

landscaping. Through 1972 the building fund campaign went on. We had a
new national chairman of fund raising in the Festival family. (He was more
family that most perhaps in that he was my brother, D'Arcy Doherty.)
While Calvin Rand continued to look after fund raising in the United States,
D'Arcy applied himself to the business of administering a campaign in
Canada that was moving swiftly on a variety of fronts. There was Lotterio, a
lottery in which several Ontario theatre, music, and opera groups
participated. There were the fine efforts of the Friends of Shaw, a volunteer
group in Toronto, led by the ever-resourceful Jeanie Hersenhoren. There
were the productive projects of the Women's Committee in Niagara. In fact,
there was so much going on that John Brook left the Festival Board to
become staff co-ordinator of fund raising. All possible donors were
approached, and gradually money was accumulated. Not a million dollars
all at once, of course, but enough to keep hopes high and construction
moving.

And our skilled troupe of actors was on the move, too, to one of
America's finest showcases for the performing arts. Early in 1972 the
company was invited to take *Misalliance* to the Eisenhower Theater of the
Kennedy Center for the Performing Arts in Washington, D.C. We were
the first foreign theatrical company to play the Eisenhower Theater.

At about the time that I was turning the first sod at the theatre site,
Paxton Whitehead was casting *Misalliance*. On May 22 it went on tour, to
Ottawa, to Rochester, New York, to Kingston and Montreal, and finally to
Washington, toward the end of June. There, as glowing notices and
enthusiastic audiences attested, we scored a triumph. Indeed we were soon
invited to take *The Philanderer* to Washington in the first weeks of 1973.

In 1972, as well as *Misalliance*, we staged *The Royal Family* and *Getting
Married*. All three played in modified repertory from June 12 to September
10. *Music Today 72* flourished. The Orford Quartet and the Lyric Trio
performed their contemporary repertoire, as well as two evenings of more

traditional music, at St Mark's Anglican Church. An unusual quintet of percussionists gave two concerts.

Each year represented a hallmark of some sort in the Festival's history, and 1972 had its own special imprint. We played to sold-out houses. The building fund, while still short of its objective, was thriving. When we needed sustenance, we had only to walk down the street to the construction site to see our dream taking shape. Paxton Whitehead summed it all up.

COURT HOUSE MEMORIES

The Court House Theatre has been the home of the Shaw Festival for eleven years. In 1972 she is making yet another of her farewell appearances. In the beginning of the Court House's theatrical history, there was a room and a small stage; then came Brian Doherty, seats, *Candida*, Equity, Andrew Allan, air conditioning (of sorts), risers, a larger stage, and Barry Morse. I knew little about those years. But the last six years hold many memories—memories that belong to the Court House and that I hope she will remember with pride. She has not been easy to work in, but the moments of achievement and triumph over adversity are what I will remember:

Playing the Interlude from *The Apple Cart* opposite the fantastic Zoe Caldwell.

The opening night of Edward Gilbert's strikingly original production of *Arms and the Man*—that was the first play under my artistic directorship—when within a short while after the play ended a thunderstorm caused the entire Niagara peninsula to be blacked out for several hours. Happily, by then we were mildly intoxicated at Calvin Rand's. Someone was watching over us that day.

Then came Jessica Tandy in Val Gielgud's *Heartbreak House* and the night the air conditioning broke down in a heat wave for several days—and we had to interrupt the second act to make another intermission and allow nearly four hundred people to breathe—but still they came.

The world première of *The Chemmy Circle*.

David Hutcheson as Sir Ralph Bloomfield Bonington convincing an opening night audience at *The Doctor's Dilemma* to believe that he had totally forgotten his lines when his next words were, 'I seem to have lost the thread of this conversation'—well, the roof nearly came in; and the poor woman in the front row who was taken ill, stopping the show—when four supposedly eminent physicians were on stage totally powerless to help her—as B.B. would say, 'She recovered, she recovered.'

Lila Kedrova in *The Guardsman* and playing a scene with her by torchlight as all the lights in Niagara had fused—another thunderstorm.

Stanley Holloway and his two-foot cigar on the closing night of *Candida* and filling in to a delighted full house with *Albert and the Lion*, *Brown Boots*, and other numbers from his days with the Co-optimists on a double bill with Tony van Bridge in excerpts from *G.K.C.* —I wondered why we bothered to mount *Candida* at all!

And then last year Carole Shelley lighting up *Tonight at 8:30* like no one since Mrs A.

But that will not be all. There is 1972—and then who knows. Fringe activities have sprung up in Niagara-on-the-Lake—the Canadian Mime Theatre, *G.K.C.*, the seminars, *Spoon River Anthology* and *Music Today*—that may well wish to use the Court House if at all possible. And there will always be a play or two that will find its 'friendly confines', if Ernie Banks will allow me to use his phrase, ideal. What other theatre building could have housed so admirably the boys of Albion House in the North American première of *Forty Years On?*

*Opening Night at the Court House
Theatre, June 1972*

1 9 7 2

THE ROYAL FAMILY
George S. Kaufman and Edna Ferber

Paul Kligman as Oscar Wolfe, Patricia Gage as Kitty Dean, Shepperd Strudwick as Herbert Dean

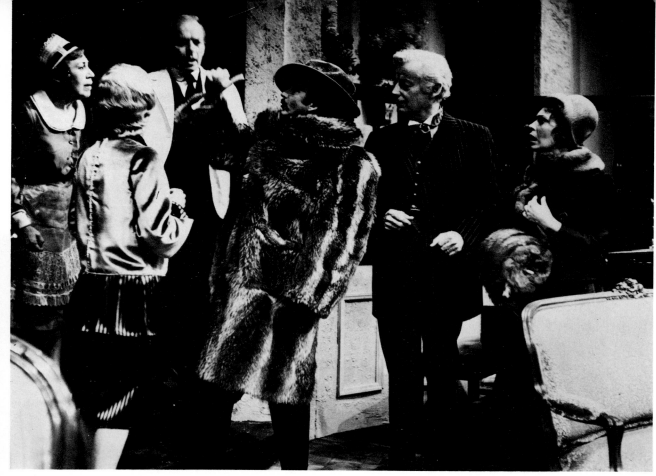

Cosette Lee as Della, Charmion King as
Julia Cavendish, Larry Reynolds as Jo, Jim
McQueen as Anthony Cavendish,
Shepperd Strudwick as Herbert Dean,
Patricia Gage as Kitty Dean

Charmion King as Julia Cavendish, Jonah
Royston as Gilbert Marshall

Charmion King as Julia Cavendish, Susan
Hogan as Gwen, Ruth Nelson as Fanny
Cavendish, Bradley Southam as Aubrey

Noel Howlett as the Bishop, Tom Kneebone as Soames, Moya Fenwick as Mrs George

GETTING MARRIED

James Valentine as Reginald Bridgenorth, 'Wenna Shaw as Leo, Susan Chapple as Lesbia, Ronald Drake as General Bridgenorth, Susan Hogan as Edith, Owen Foran as Collins, Heath Lamberts as Sinjon Hotchkiss
Moya Fenwick as Mrs George, Michael Hogan as Cecil Sykes, Pat Roberto as the Beadle, Betty Leighton as Mrs Bridgenorth, Noel Howlett as the Bishop, Tom Kneebone as Soames

*Heath Lamberts as Sinjon Hotchkiss,
'Wenna Shaw as Leo, James Valentine as
Reginald Bridgenorth*

MISALLIANCE

. . . "Misalliance" opened last night at the Eisenhower Theater. The production, by the Shaw Festival from Niagara-on-the-Lake, Canada, is gorgeous, not a trick missed anywhere.

The players are superb, the setting and costumes imaginative and appropriate. The play itself is top-quality Shaw. . . .

The key contribution, of course, is Paxton Whitehead's nimble direction, with movement enhancing and revealing the flow of thought, never obscuring it. The director serves Shaw as well as the playwright serves his audience.

Frank Getlein
The Evening Star, Washington, D.C.

James Valentine as Joseph Percival, Angela Wood as Lina Szczepanowska

Angela Wood as Lina Szczepanowska,
Ronald Drake as Mr Tarleton

Heath Lamberts as 'Gunner'

. . . Mr. Lamberts is hard to describe:
imagine a bowl of jello putting on airs,
yet about to burst into tears at any
moment. He is one rotund tremor of
fear and puppy fat, playing scales of
hysteria at varied volumes on his voice,
and playing every comic stunt stage
tradition has sanctified for nervous
gunsels: cocking his revolver only to
have the front half fall down, etc. . . .
His performance is a real stage creation;
he manages to travel the main lines of
Shaw's speeches, but gives you a
recognizable and comic human being in
between them.

Michael Feingold
The Village Voice, New York, N.Y.

*Noel Howlett as Lord Summerhays,
'Wenna Shaw as Hypatia Tarleton*

. . . the "Misalliance" of a lifetime. . . .
R. P. Harriss
The News American, Baltimore, Md.

*Noel Howlett as Lord Summerhays, Betty
Leighton as Mrs Tarleton, Ronald Drake as
Mr Tarleton, Angela Wood as Lina
Szczepanowska*
*Malcolm Armstrong as Johnny Tarleton,
'Wenna Shaw as Hypatia Tarleton, James
Valentine as Joseph Percival, Tom
Kneebone as Bentley Summerhays*

121

*Betty Leighton as Mrs Tarleton, Malcolm
Armstrong as Johnny Tarleton, Tom
Kneebone as Bentley Summerhays, 'Wenna
Shaw as Hypatia Tarleton*

Paxton Whitehead as Leonard Charteris,
Patricia Gage as Julia Craven

123

. . . Canada's Shaw Festival last night inaugurated the new year at the Eisenhower Theater with this satire [*The Philanderer*] which focuses on The New Woman of the '90s in an aware, stylish production that gives one the happy illusion of seeing a new play by Shaw—not, to be sure, major Shaw—but a play of enormously amusing interest. . . .

Patricia Gage is spiritedly outraged as the ungentle Julia and Charlotte Blunt contrasts her with a cool, blond grace as the thank-you-no-thanks Grace.

Whitehead's Philanderer is a marvelously bravura performance. The actor licks his chops over the slightest phrases or pauses to take us with him into Shaw's thoughts. The physical likeness not only furthers the fun, but does so honorably, for Shaw wrote of himself.

Maurice Strike's swiftly accommodating settings and the costumes of Tiina Lipp bring the final assurance of just the right style for a comedy which seems stylishly witty and assured. No, not major Shaw, but unfamiliar Shaw with a surprising freshness.

Richard L. Coe, *The Washington Post*
Washington, D.C.

Standing: Paxton Whitehead as Leonard Charteris, 'Wenna Shaw as Sylvia Craven, Patrick Boxill as Colonel Craven, Sandy Webster as Joseph Cuthbertson
Foreground: Patricia Gage as Julia Craven, Charlotte Blunt as Grace Tranfield, James Valentine as Dr Paramore

SHAW IN THE NEW THEATRE

Peter Smith is neither actor, nor director, nor member of the Festival staff, but through 1972 and the early months of 1973 he was essential to the Festival. Peter was Ron Thom's man on the job, the project architect for the new theatre. He handled the knotty problems of construction and held to deadlines. And we worried about those deadlines, especially when by January 1973 we had chalked up $90,000 in advance bookings—the biggest advance sale in our history.

It was a near thing. By the first week of May, the administrative and production staffs were able to move into their new quarters, but the rehearsal halls and the stage weren't ready. There were no seats in the auditorium, no lighting, no curtain. And there was a monumental job of landscaping still to be done. The weather seemed to conspire against us. All through the month of May it rained. To add to the soggy mess, the Niagara Works Department was in the process of re-laying the road in front of the theatre.

We needed a miracle and we seemed to get it. Toward the end of the month the Works Department withdrew, leaving behind a smooth new road. From what a few weeks earlier had seemed a swamp, there began to emerge a green and graceful park in just the shape and form Ron Thom's drawings and models had forecast. Inside the theatre the work was completed, and Ray Senior and his young assistants hung their hand-woven curtain. Even so, at noon on the opening day there was still some sod to be laid round the reflecting pool and there were still a few bricks to be placed along the entrance driveway.

*The final twenty-four hours before the
official opening of the new Shaw Festival
Theatre, June 1973*

Tom Burrows, with the help of Judith Hendry, Beverley Mitchell, Linda Rettig, Gail Legate, and Jeanie Hersenhoren had assembled and co-ordinated guest lists for seven opening nights, a state visit, and a special performance for the Queen. Volunteers for Shaw, a special committee headed by Betty Mitchell, had planned parties, accommodation, and hospitality for the special guests. The Women's Committee, led by Jean

Gent and Lillian Magder, were planning daily tours of the new theatre for all visitors to the Shaw Festival.

Right on schedule the inaugural week began. It was to be a magic week. On stage there was *You Never Can Tell* and on four afternoons the Orford Quartet, the Canadian Brass with the Canadian Mime Theatre, and the National Arts Centre orchestra. Off stage there was a gay round of parties, dinners, and champagne receptions, which spread from the theatre to the homes of the Festival directors and their friends. Rarely had Niagara-on-the-Lake revelled in such an atmosphere of festivity.

There were celebrities, dignitaries, and world leaders. Prime Minister Trudeau visited the Festival with Prime Minister Indira Gandhi of India, who was his guest at the time. Premier William Davis and Lieutenant-Governor Ross Macdonald of Ontario came. And as a climax to that early round of special events, Her Majesty Queen Elizabeth II and His Royal Highness the Duke of Edinburgh attended a special performance of *You Never Can Tell*. They reached Niagara-on-the-Lake after an exhausting day of eighteen visits to other parts of Ontario, but they stayed through the entire performance and went backstage to meet the cast.

For the inaugural season Paxton Whitehead mounted a program of three plays: *You Never Can Tell, The Brass Butterfly*, and *Fanny's First Play*. They kept the new house packed with delighted audiences. 'Another struggle begins,' Paxton said at the beginning of the first year in the new theatre. 'Another struggle—living up to our own expectations and our author.'

No one could speak for George Bernard Shaw, who could never have dreamed of a Shaw Festival in Niagara-on-the-Lake, but there were many voices raised on behalf of the Festival company. It was Stanley Holloway, reflecting on the new theatre before opening night, who said: 'There are no laughs or applause soaked into the walls yet. We've got to put those in.' That first season made a beginning.

THE NEW SHAW FESTIVAL THEATRE

. . . Beautifully proportioned and
superbly detailed, the new Shaw
Festival Theatre gives its lucky
audiences room to admire, room to
wander and, most important, room to
think. It is an environment which leaves
a dimension for the intellect, for words,
ideas and reflection. . . .

The Toronto Star

*The outdoor terrace and the lobbies where
theatregoers gather before the play and
between the acts*

. . . Now, in its 12th season, the Shaw festival last week played its trump card. It is a new 830-seat theater, and it is one of the loveliest in North America. Designed by the Canadian architect R.J. Thom, it has avoided almost all of the pitfalls of contemporary theater architecture. Brick outside, cedar wood inside and carefully landscaped into its environment, the theater is cozy and inviting. The sightlines seem admirable, the acoustics at least fair, back-stage facilities are well spoken of by dispassionate professionals, and the proscenium-style house is a perfect joy. . . .

Clive Barnes, *The New York Times*

THE OFFICIAL OPENING

A Shaw Festival tradition on opening nights: the Welland Police Club Pipes and Drums

Premier William G. Davis of Ontario and Mrs Davis, Mr and Mrs Calvin Rand being escorted to the inaugural performance by Warrant Officer Platt of the Royal Regiment of Canada.

Thomas Burrows, Premier William G.
Davis and Mrs Davis, Mr and Mrs Calvin
Rand, and Brian Doherty

The Hon.Robert Welch, Premier William
G. Davis, and Calvin Rand in an on-stage
ceremony commemorating the gift of
$500,000 from the Government of Ontario
to the Shaw Festival

Festival Board member Harry Tomarin with R. J. Thom, Shaw Festival Theatre architect, and Mrs Thom

First night guests Mr Edward Regan, County Executive of Erie County, New York, and Mrs Regan

FOUNDER'S DAY

Lieutenant-Governor of Ontario Ross Macdonald with Brian Doherty

THE TRUDEAU VISIT

Prime Minister Pierre Trudeau and Mrs Trudeau, with Prime Minister Indira Gandhi of India, arriving for the Critics' Night performance of You Never Can Tell, *June 20, 1973*

Prime Minister Trudeau accepting a plaque acknowledging the gift of $500,000 from the Government of Canada to the Shaw Festival

Board Secretary Dorothy Middleditch with Prime Minister Indira Gandhi

Prime Minister and Mrs Trudeau with Brian Doherty

THE ROYAL VISIT

A special performance marking the visit of Her Majesty the Queen and His Royal Highness the Duke of Edinburgh to the Shaw Festival Theatre, Niagara-on-the-Lake, June 28, 1973

Her Majesty the Queen and His Royal Highness the Duke of Edinburgh arriving at the theatre escorted by Thomas Burrows, Jake Froese, Lord Mayor of Niagara-on-the-Lake, Mrs Calvin Rand, Mrs Thomas Burrows, and Brian Doherty

In the Royal Box

Artistic Director Paxton Whitehead escorts Her Majesty the Queen backstage to greet the cast of You Never Can Tell

The Royal Party departing through the theatre foyer

YOU NEVER CAN TELL

Peter Blais as Philip Clandon, Stanley Holloway as the Waiter, 'Wenna Shaw as Dorothy Clandon

Norman Welsh as Fergus Crampton, Stanley Holloway as the Waiter

You can always tell about "You Never Can Tell." If well and truly played, George Bernard Shaw's 1896 comedy of family matters and manners emerges as a marvelously fresh, mellow, cheerful, and witty entertainment. Well and truly played it is in the revival which opened the Shaw Festival's 12th season and inaugurated its new $3 million playhouse.

The elegant production staged by Edward Gilbert—with sets by Maurice Strike and costumes by Hilary Corbett—abounds in an airiness ideally suited to a comedy set at an English seaside resort. . . .

John Beaufort
The Christian Science Monitor,
Boston, Mass.

143

Paxton Whitehead as Valentine, Patrick Boxill as Finch M'Comas, James Valentine as Bohun, Mary Savidge as Mrs Lanfrey Clandon, Norman Welsh as Fergus Crampton, Patricia Gage as Gloria Clandon

Patrick Boxill as Finch M'Comas, James Valentine as Bohun, Peter Blais as Philip Clandon, 'Wenna Shaw as Dorothy Clandon, Norman Welsh as Fergus Crampton

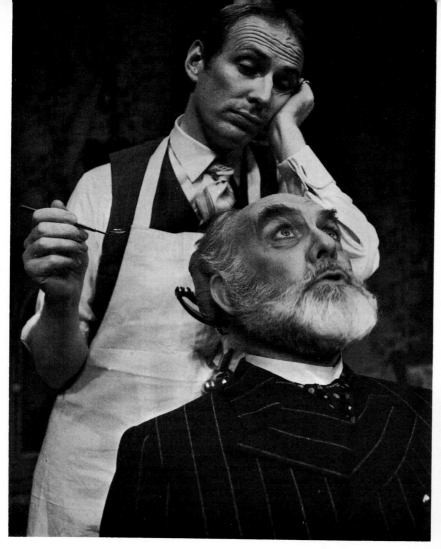

Paxton Whitehead as Valentine, Norman Welsh as Fergus Crampton

Patricia Gage as Gloria Clandon, Norman Welsh as Fergus Crampton

THE BRASS BUTTERFLY
William Golding

John Swindells as Captain of the Guard,
August Schellenberg as Postumus,
Stephen Markle as Mamillius

Melody Horbulyk as Euphrosyne,
Lockwood West as the Emperor

James Valentine as Phanocles, Stephen Markle as Mamillius, Lockwood West as the Emperor

FANNY'S FIRST PLAY

Paxton Whitehead as Cecil Savoyard,
Maynard Burgess as the Footman

Mary Savidge as Mrs Knox, Domini
Blythe as Margaret Knox, Gerard Parkes as ▷
Mr Knox, August Schellenberg as
Duvallet

Domini Blythe as Margaret Knox, Blair Brown as Fanny O'Dowda

Domini Blythe as Margaret Knox, 'Wenna Shaw as Dora Delaney, Stephen Markle as Bobby Gilbey

Marjorie Le Strange as Mrs Gilbey, Alan Nunn as Robin Gilbey

Alan Nunn as Robin Gilbey, 'Wenna Shaw as Dora Delaney, James Valentine as Juggins

CAST AND COMPANY LISTS

1962

8-performance 'Salute to Shaw'

'Don Juan in Hell' from *Man and Superman*

Don Juan	David Loveless
Doña Ana	Mavis Corser
The Statue	Eric Davis
The Devil	Maynard Burgess

Directed by Maynard Burgess

CANDIDA

Prossy	Jean Malloy
Morell	David Michener
Lexy	Terry Cahill
Burgess	Edward Fordham
Candida	Barbara Ransom
Marchbanks	Tim Devlin

Directed by Maynard Burgess
Sets designed by Alice Crawley
Costumes designed by Louis G. Berai

1963

3-week season

YOU NEVER CAN TELL

Dorothy Clandon	Mary Barton
Valentine	Sean Mulcahy
Parlourmaid	Maggie Smith
Philip Clandon	Roy Wordsworth
Mrs Lanfrey Clandon	Juliana Saxton
Gloria Clandon	Margaret Griffin
Fergus Crampton	James Edmond
Finch M'Comas	Alfred Gallagher
Waiter	Gerard Parkes
Jo	James Beggs
Bohun	Ian Thorne

Directed by Andrew Allan
Designed by Martha Mann

HOW HE LIED TO HER HUSBAND

Henry	Michael Tabbitt
Aurora	Denise Ferguson
Teddy	James Edmond

THE MAN OF DESTINY

Giuseppe	Guy Sanvido
Napoleon Bonaparte	Ian Thorne
Sub-Lieutenant	James Beggs
The Strange Lady	Margaret Griffin

Directed by Andrew Allan
Designed by Martha Mann

ANDROCLES AND THE LION

The Lion	James Beggs
Androcles	Maynard Burgess
Megaera	Barbara Spigel
The Centurion	Gerard Parkes
The Captain	Ian Thorne
Lavinia	Denise Ferguson
Lentulus	Roy Wordsworth
Metellus	Michael Tabbitt
Ferrovius	Percy Rodriguez
Spintho	Guy Sanvido
Ox-Driver	Lowell Patterson
Secutor	Alastair Summerfield
Retiarius	Ian Gent
Call Boy	Roger Picken
The Editor	Alfred Gallagher
Menagerie Keeper	Lowell Patterson
The Emperor	Andrew Allan
Trumpeter	Brian Yanik
Christians	Corinna Bruce, Bonnie Bowering, Jennifer Brunton, Sandy Clair, Margo Fyfe, Heather Fyfe, Barbara Harrison, Pam Hiscott, Jean Herzog, Ann Hustleby, Lyn Munroe, Robin Rand, Betty Robertson
Roman Soldiers	Roderick Brennan, Eddie Yates, W. W. Blue
Gladiators	Vincent Burt, Gary Middleditch

Directed by Sean Mulcahy
Designed by Martha Mann

1964

4-week season

HEARTBREAK HOUSE

Ellie Dunn	Mary Benning
Nurse Guinness	Joyce Campion
Captain Shotover	Norman Welsh
Lady Utterword	Betty Leighton
Hesione Hushabye	Moya Fenwick
Mazzini Dunn	Alfred Gallagher
Hector Hushabye	Christopher Newton
Boss Mangan	Robert Hewitt
Randall Utterword	Michael Tabbitt
Burglar	Donald Ewer

Directed by Andrew Allan
Designed by Lawrence Schafer
Lighting designed by Donald Acaster

VILLAGE WOOING

Miss 'Z'	Linda Livingston
Mr 'A'	Christopher Newton
Deck Steward	W. W. Blue

Directed by Sean Mulcahy
Designed by Lawrence Schafer
Lighting designed by Donald Acaster

THE DARK LADY OF THE SONNETS

The Beefeater	Donald Ewer
William Shakespear	Jack Medley
Queen Elizabeth I	Moya Fenwick
The Dark Lady	Linda Livingston

Directed by Sean Mulcahy
Designed by Lawrence Schafer
Lighting designed by Donald Acaster

JOHN BULL'S OTHER ISLAND

Tom Broadbent	Paul Craig
Hodson	Leo Phillips
Tim Haffigan	Michael Tabbitt
Larry Doyle	Sean Mulcahy
Peter Keegan	Gerard Parkes
Patsy Farrell	Lawrence Beattie
Nora Reilly	Mary Benning
Father Dempsey	Alfred Gallagher
Cornelius Doyle	Michael Snow
Aunt Judy	Joyce Campion
Matthew Haffigan	Leo Leyden
Barney Doran	John W. McMullan
Barney Doran's Friends	W. W. Blue,

Roger Picken, Michael Tabbitt, Terry Tweed, Mary Welsman

Directed by Andrew Allan
Designed by Lawrence Schafer
Lighting designed by Donald Acaster

1965

6-week season

PYGMALION

Clara Eynsford-Hill	Mary Barton
Mrs Eynsford-Hill	Joyce Campion
Independent Bystander	Randolph Rhodes
Freddy Eynsford-Hill	Howard Lever
Eliza Doolittle	Anne Butler
Colonel Pickering	Alfred Gallagher
Henry Higgins	Paul Craig
Sarcastic Bystander	Norman Harding
Mrs Pearce	Betty Leighton
Alfred Doolittle	Gerard Parkes
Mrs Higgins	Juliana Saxton
The Parlourmaid	Jean Stainer
People in Covent Garden	Elaine Freeman,

W. W. Blue, Joan Huggins, Jane McEwan, Susan McEwan, Roger Picken

Directed by Andrew Allan
Designed by Lawrence Schafer
Lighting designed by Donald Acaster

THE SHADOW OF A GUNMAN by Sean O'Casey

Donal Davoren	Sean Mulcahy
Seumas Shields	Gerard Parkes
Mr Maguire	Laurence Seigel
Mr Mulligan	John W. McMullan
Minnie Powell	Nuala Fitzgerald
Tommy Owens	Michael Snow
Mrs Henderson	Marie Pringle
Mr Gallogher	Alfred Gallagher
Mrs Grigson	Joyce Campion
Adolphus Grigson	Lawrence Beattie
An Auxiliary (Black and Tan)	Paul Craig

Directed by Sean Mulcahy
Designed by Lawrence Schafer
Lighting designed by Donald Acaster

THE MILLIONAIRESS

Julius Sagamore	Sean Mulcahy
Epifania Ognisanti di Pareria	Anne Butler
Alastair Fitzfassenden	Paul Craig
Patricia Smith	Mary Barton
Adrian Blenderbland	Alfred Gallagher
The Doctor	Roger Dauphin
The Sweatshop Man	Michael Snow
The Sweatshop Woman	Betty Leighton
The Hotel Manager	Howard Lever

Directed by Andrew Allan
Designed by Lawrence Schafer
Lighting designed by Donald Acaster

1966

9-week season

MAN AND SUPERMAN

Roebuck Ramsden	Norman Welsh
Parlourmaid	Janet Gladish
Octavius Robinson	Paxton Whitehead
John Tanner	Barry Morse
Ann Whitefield	Pat Galloway
Mrs Whitefield	Betty Leighton
Miss Ramsden	Molly Hancock
Violet Robinson	Susan Clark
Henry Straker	Tom Kneebone
Hector Malone	Paul Craig
Mendoza	Hugh Webster
Mr Malone	Leslie Yeo
Brigands and Soldiers	Michael Bain,

Stephen Boal, Bill Bye, James Cull, Tim Hanson, Norman Harding, Grant Hawes, Roger Ivey, John Lubeck, Ellen Pierce, Tom Rosser

Directed by Barry Morse
Designed by Lawrence Schafer
Lighting designed by Donald Acaster

MISALLIANCE

Johnny Tarleton	Paul Craig
Bentley Summerhays	Tom Kneebone
Hypatia Tarleton	Susan Clark
Mrs Tarleton	Betty Leighton
Lord Summerhays	Paxton Whitehead
Mr Tarleton	Leslie Yeo
Joseph Percival	Michael Bradshaw
Lina Szczepanowska	Zoe Caldwell
'Gunner'	Howard Lever

Directed by Barry Morse
Designed by Lawrence Schafer
Lighting designed by Donald Acaster

THE APPLE CART

Pamphilius	Michael Bradshaw
Sempronius	Howard Lever
Boanerges	Henry Ramer
Magnus	Paxton Whitehead
The Princess Royal	Judy Holmes
Proteus	Patrick Boxill
Nicobar	Paul Craig
Crassus	Alfred Gallagher
Pliny	Sandy Webster
Balbus	Jon Granik
Amanda	Sheila Haney
Lysistrata	Margaret MacLeod
Orinthia	Zoe Caldwell
Queen Jemima	Betty Leighton
Mr Vanhattan	Percy Rodriguez*

*Replaced during run by Franz Russell

Directed by Edward Gilbert
Designed by Lawrence Schafer
Lighting designed by Donald Acaster

1967

9-week season

Post-season tour of *Major Barbara* to Expo 67 and Winnipeg

ARMS AND THE MAN

Catherine Petkoff	Betty Leighton
Raina Petkoff	Martha Henry
Louka	Suzanne Grossmann
Captain Bluntschli	Douglas Rain
The Russian Officer	Detlef Berthelsen
Nicola	Heath Lamberts
Major Petkoff	Sandy Webster
Major Sergius Saranoff	Paxton Whitehead

Directed by Edward Gilbert
Sets designed by Maurice Strike
Costumes designed by Hilary Corbett
Lighting designed by Christopher Root

THE CIRCLE by W. Somerset Maugham

Arnold Champion-Cheney, M.P.	Steven Sutherland
A Butler	Norman Harding
Mrs Shenstone	Margaret MacLeod
Elizabeth	Susan Ringwood
Edward Luton	Paul Collins
Clive Champion-Cheney	Hiram Sherman
Lady Catherine Champion-Cheney	Kate Reid
Lord Porteous	Leslie Yeo
A Tweenie	Pamela Brook

Directed by Paxton Whitehead
Sets designed by Maurice Strike
Costumes designed by Hilary Corbett
Lighting designed by Christopher Root

MAJOR BARBARA

Lady Britomart Undershaft	Renée Asherson
Stephen Undershaft	Thomas Clark
Morrison	Ian Downie
Sarah Undershaft	Margot Gillies
Barbara Undershaft	Irena Mayeska
Adolphus Cusins	Paxton Whitehead
Charles Lomax	Steven Sutherland
Andrew Undershaft	Larry Gates
Rummy Mitchens	Jennifer Phipps
Snobby Price	Eric House
Jenny Hill	Deborah Kipp
Peter Shirley	Patrick Boxill
Bill Walker	Roy Cooper
Mrs Baines	Margaret MacLeod
Bilton	James Cull

Directed by Edward Gilbert
Designed by Maurice Strike
Lighting designed by Christopher Root

1968

9-week season

HEARTBREAK HOUSE

Nurse Guinness	Eleanor Beecroft
Ellie Dunn	Diana LeBlanc
Captain Shotover	Tony van Bridge
Lady Utterword	Frances Hyland
Hesione Hushabye	Jessica Tandy
Mazzini Dunn	Patrick Boxill
Hector Hushabye	Paxton Whitehead
Boss Mangan	Bill Fraser
Randall Utterword	James Valentine
Burglar	Kenneth Wickes

Directed by Val Gielgud
Sets designed by Maurice Strike
Costumes designed by Hilary Corbett
Lighting designed by Donald Acaster

THE IMPORTANCE OF BEING OSCAR

Micheál MacLiammóir

The production designed and directed by Hilton Edwards

THE CHEMMY CIRCLE

Translation by Suzanne Grossmann
From *La Main Passe* by Georges Feydeau

Chanal	John Horton
Fédot	James Valentine
Hubertin	Jack Creley
Coustouillu	Paxton Whitehead
Planteloup	Patrick Boxill
Belgence	Kenneth Dight
Etienne	Kenneth Wickes
Auguste	Gary McKeehan
LaPige	James Cull
Germal	Norman Harding
Francine Chanal	Frances Hyland
Sophie Fédot	Patricia Gage
Cecille	Sandy Nicholls
Madeleine	Margot Sweeney

Directed by Paxton Whitehead
Sets designed by Joseph Cselenyi
Costumes designed by Hilary Corbett
Lighting designed by Donald Acaster

1969

10-week season

Post-season tour of *The Guardsman* to Ottawa

THE DOCTOR'S DILEMMA

The Young Man	Malcolm Armstrong
Emmy	Gertrude Bradley
Sir Colenso Ridgeon	Robert Flemyng
Leo Schutzmacher	Sam Moses
Sir Patrick Cullen	James Edmond
Cutler Walpole	Kenneth Dight
Sir Ralph Bloomfield Bonington	David Hutcheson
Blenkinsop	Patrick Boxill
Jennifer Dubedat	Helen Finn
Louis Dubedat	Paxton Whitehead
Minnie Tinwell	Sylvia Feigel

Directed by Dillon Evans
Sets designed by James Tilton
Costumes designed by Hilary Corbett
Lighting designed by Donald Acaster

BACK TO METHUSELAH Part I

Adam	Jonathan White
Eve	Frances Hyland
The Serpent	Barbara Chilcott
Cain	Roland Hewgill

Conceived and directed by Marigold Charlesworth
Designed by Les Lawrence
Music composed and directed by Eugene Martynec
Original song composed and played by the Kensington Market
Environmental lighting and special effects by Catharsis *in collaboration with* Donald Acaster

FIVE VARIATIONS FOR CORNO DI BASSETTO

Corno di Bassetto	John Horton
Compère	Patrick Boxill
Musicians	Mary Simmons, Soprano;

Reginald Godden, Piano; Gerard Kantarjian, Violin; Albin Berky, Cello; Jay Morton, Clarinet

Arranged by Louis Applebaum *and* Ronald Hambleton
Staged by Patrick Boxill

THE GUARDSMAN by Ferenc Molnár

English version by Frank Marcus

The Actress, Ilona	Lila Kedrova
The Actor, Nandor	Paxton Whitehead
The Critic, Bela	Carl Don
The 'Mother'	Hanna Sarvasova
The Maid, Liesl	Susan King
The Creditor, Rosenzweig	Tibor Feheregyhazi
The Usherette, Mrs Nagy	Molly Rutledge*
The Cook	Margot Sweeney

*Played by Trudi Renés in Ottawa
Directed by Stephen Porter
Sets designed by Maurice Strike
Costumes designed by Tiina Lipp
Lighting designed by Donald Acaster

1970

11-week season

Pre-season tour of *Candida* to Ottawa and Kingston

CANDIDA

Prossy	Jennifer Phipps
Morell	Tony van Bridge
Lexy	Leslie Carlson
Burgess	Stanley Holloway
Candida	Frances Hyland
Marchbanks	Chris Sarandon*

*Replaced for final week by Donald Warfield
Directed by Harris Yulin
Sets designed by Maurice Strike
Costumes designed by Hilary Corbett
Lighting designed by Gil Wechsler

G.K.C.

The Wit and Wisdom of Gilbert Keith Chesterton

Compiled, arranged, and played by Tony van Bridge
Direction assistance by Frances Hyland

FORTY YEARS ON by Alan Bennett

Headmaster	Robert Harris
Franklin	Alan Scarfe
Tempest	Paxton Whitehead
Matron	Jennifer Phipps
Miss Nisbitt	Amelia Hall
Organist	Peter Orme
The Boys of Albion House	Peter Bennett,

David Eden, Roy Hopper, Glen Kotyk, Stephen Lane, Richard Lawrence, Ian MacLaren, Evan McCowan, John Nicholl, Peter Pilgrim, Tim Pilgrim, Nicholas Pope, Christopher Szczucinski, Michael Thompson, Thomas Weld, Reid Willis, Alexander Willows

Directed by Paxton Whitehead
Set designed by Maurice Strike
Costumes designed by Tiina Lipp *and* Reg Samuel
Lighting designed by Gil Wechsler

1971

12-week season

Pre-season tour of *The Philanderer* to Ottawa, Kingston, Montreal, and Rochester, N.Y.

THE PHILANDERER

Leonard Charteris	Paxton Whitehead
Grace Tranfield	Patricia Collins
Julia Craven	Louise Marleau*
Joseph Cuthbertson	Norman Welsh
Colonel Craven	Patrick Boxill
Dr Paramore	James Valentine
Sylvia Craven	Diana Barrington
Page	Glen Kotyk

Pages Robert Freeman, Jerrold Karch, Christopher Toye

*Played in Ottawa and Montreal by Patricia Gage

Directed by Tony van Bridge
Sets designed by Maurice Strike
Costumes designed by Tiina Lipp
Lighting designed by Donald Acaster

SUMMER DAYS by Romain Weingarten

Translated by Suzanne Grossmann

Simon	Derek McGrath
Semi-Succotash	Eric House
Lorette	Nancy Beatty
Lord Garlic	Jack Creley

Directed by Michael Bawtree
Designed by Brian Jackson
Music by Poldi Shaetzman
Lighting designed by Donald Acaster

TONIGHT AT 8:30 by Noel Coward

We Were Dancing

Ippaga	Derek McGrath
George Davies	James Valentine
Eva Blake	Susan Hogan
Louise Charteris	Carole Shelley
Karl Sandys	Paxton Whitehead
Hubert Charteris	Hiram Sherman
Clara Bethel	Barbara Hamilton
Major Blake	Michael Hogan

Family Album

Jasper Featherways	Hiram Sherman
Jane (his wife)	Carole Shelley
Lavinia Featherways	Barbara Hamilton
Richard Featherways	Derek McGrath
Harriet Winter	Nancy Beatty
Charles Winter	Michael Hogan
Emily Valance	Susan Hogan
Edward Valance	Paxton Whitehead
Burrows	Patrick Boxill

Shadow Play

Lena	Nancy Beatty
Victoria Gayforth	Carole Shelley
Martha Cunningham	Barbara Hamilton
Simon Gayforth	Paxton Whitehead
Hodge	Derek McGrath
Sibyl Heston	Susan Hogan
Michael Doyle	Michael Hogan
A Young Man	James Valentine
George Cunningham	Hiram Sherman
At the Piano	Peter Orme, Lynne Honsberger

Directed by Eric House
Sets designed by Maurice Strike
Costumes designed by Hilary Corbett
Lighting designed by Donald Acaster
Music directed and arranged by Peter Orme

WAR, WOMEN AND OTHER TRIVIA

A Social Success by Max Beerbohm

Tommy Dixon	James Valentine
Duchess of Huntington	Barbara Hamilton
Earl of Amersham	Hiram Sherman
Henry Robbins	Eric House
Countess of Amersham	Susan Hogan
Hawkins	Derek McGrath

Directed by Patrick Boxill
Designed by Maurice Strike
Lighting designed by Donald Acaster

O'Flaherty, V.C.

O'Flaherty	Michael Hogan
Sir Pearce	Patrick Boxill
Mrs O'Flaherty	Barbara Hamilton
Teresa	Susan Hogan

Directed by Patrick Boxill
Sets designed by Maurice Strike
Costumes designed by Hilary Corbett
Lighting designed by Donald Acaster

Press Cuttings

General Mitchener	James Valentine
Orderly	Eric House
Balsquith	Patrick Boxill
Mrs Farrell	Nancy Beatty
Mrs Banger	Barbara Hamilton
Lady Corinthia	Carole Shelley

Directed by Paxton Whitehead
Sets designed by Maurice Strike
Costumes designed by Hilary Corbett
Lighting designed by Donald Acaster

157

1972

13-week season

Pre-season tour of *Misalliance* to Ottawa, Kingston, Montreal, Rochester, N.Y., and Washington, D.C.

THE ROYAL FAMILY
By George S. Kaufman and Edna Ferber

Della	Cosette Lee
Jo	Larry Reynolds
Hallboys	Peter Kufluk, Alexander Willows
McDermott	Jonathan White
Herbert Dean	Shepperd Strudwick
Kitty Dean	Patricia Gage
Gwen	Susan Hogan
Perry Stewart	Michael Hogan
Fanny Cavendish	Ruth Nelson
Oscar Wolfe	Paul Kligman
Julia Cavendish	Charmion King
Anthony Cavendish	Jim McQueen
Gilbert Marshall	Jonah Royston
Miss Peake	Betty Thompson
Chauffeur	Tom Strawford
Gunga	MacCowan Thomas
Aubrey	Bradley Southam

Directed by Donald Davis
Sets designed by Tom Doherty
Costumes designed by Hilary Corbett
Lighting designed by Donald Acaster

MISALLIANCE

Johnny Tarleton	Malcolm Armstrong
Bentley Summerhays	Tom Kneebone*
Hypatia Tarleton	'Wenna Shaw
Mrs Tarleton	Betty Leighton
Lord Summerhays	Noel Howlett
Mr Tarleton	Ronald Drake
Joseph Percival	James Valentine
Lina Szczepanowska	Angela Wood
'Gunner'	Heath Lamberts

*Replaced by Robin Marshall in September
Directed by Paxton Whitehead
Sets designed by Maurice Strike
Costumes designed by Hilary Corbett
Lighting designed by Lynne Hyde

GETTING MARRIED

Mrs Bridgenorth	Betty Leighton
Collins	Owen Foran
General Bridgenorth	Ronald Drake
Lesbia	Susan Chapple
Reginald Bridgenorth	James Valentine
Leo	'Wenna Shaw
The Bishop	Noel Howlett
Sinjon Hotchkiss	Heath Lamberts
Cecil Sykes	Michael Hogan
Edith	Susan Hogan
Soames	Tom Kneebone
The Beadle	Pat Roberto
Mrs George	Moya Fenwick

Directed by Paxton Whitehead
Sets designed by Maurice Strike
Costumes designed by Judy Peyton-Ward
Lighting designed by Al Anderson

1973

15-week season

January engagement of *The Philanderer* for two weeks at the John F. Kennedy Center for the Performing Arts, Washington, D.C.

Post-season tour of *You Never Can Tell* to Ottawa; Winnipeg; Detroit, Michigan; New Haven, Connecticut; and Ann Arbor, Michigan

THE PHILANDERER

Leonard Charteris	Paxton Whitehead
Grace Tranfield	Charlotte Blunt
Julia Craven	Patricia Gage
Joseph Cuthbertson	Sandy Webster
Colonel Craven	Patrick Boxill
Dr Paramore	James Valentine
Sylvia Craven	'Wenna Shaw
Page	Christopher Gladstone

Directed by Tony van Bridge
Sets designed by Maurice Strike
Costumes designed by Tiina Lipp
Lighting designed by Donald Acaster

YOU NEVER CAN TELL

Dorothy Clandon	'Wenna Shaw
Valentine	Paxton Whitehead
Parlourmaid	Melody Horbulyk[*1]
Philip Clandon	Peter Blais
Mrs Lanfrey Clandon	Mary Savidge[*2]
Gloria Clandon	Patricia Gage
Fergus Crampton	Norman Welsh[*3]
Finch M'Comas	Patrick Boxill
Waiter	Stanley Holloway[*4]
Jo	Howard Hughes
Cook	Betty Thompson
Bohun	James Valentine

[*1]*Replaced for tour by Janet Doherty and Margaret Lamb*
[*2]*Replaced for tour (after Ottawa) by Sheila Haney*
[*3]*Replaced for school performances and tour by Richard Farrell*
[*4]*Replaced for school performances and tour by Richard Murdoch*

Directed by Edward Gilbert
Sets designed by Maurice Strike
Costumes designed by Hilary Corbett
Lighting designed by Donald Acaster

THE BRASS BUTTERFLY by William Golding

Mamillius	Stephen Markle
Captain of the Guard	John Swindells
Postumus	August Schellenberg
Emperor	Lockwood West
Phanocles	James Valentine
Euphrosyne	Melody Horbulyk
A Sergeant	Chris Kelk
Attendants	Carol Crawford, Hollis McClaren,

Milton Branton, Simon Briand, Klaus Gorges,
Howard Hughes
Directed by Joseph Shaw
Sets designed by Brian Jackson
Costumes designed by John Fenney
Lighting designed by Donald Acaster

FANNY'S FIRST PLAY

The Audience

A Footman	Maynard Burgess
Count O'Dowda	Maury Cooper
Cecil Savoyard	Paxton Whitehead
Fanny O'Dowda	Blair Brown

The Critics

Mr Trotter	Patrick Boxill
Mr Vaughan	John Swindells
Mr Gunn	Chris Kelk
Mr Flawner Bannal	Howard Hughes

The Players

Billy Burjoyce	Peter Kufluk
Robin Gilbey	Alan Nunn
Mrs Gilbey	Marjorie Le Strange
Juggins	James Valentine
Dora Delaney	'Wenna Shaw
Mrs Knox	Mary Savidge
Mr Knox	Gerard Parkes
Margaret Knox	Domini Blythe
Bobby Gilbey	Stephen Markle
Mr Duvallet	August Schellenberg

Directed by Brian Murray
Sets designed by Maurice Strike
Costumes designed by Hilary Corbett
Lighting designed by Donald Acaster

PRODUCTION STAFF 1973

Katherine Robertson
Joseph Glosson
Production Stage Managers

Al Anderson
Technical Director

Ron Nipper
Stage Manager

David Bunyan
Assistant Stage Manager

Max Bartel
House Carpenter

Andy Saelens
House Electrician

David R. Dague
Prop Maker

Pat MacKenzie
Design Assistant

Werner Kulovits
Cutter

Olive Etwarroo
First Wardrobe Assistant

Patricia Bentley
Wardrobe Assistant

Mary-Ann Wilson
Wardrobe Assistant

Margaret Lamb
Wardrobe Mistress

Laurie Freeman
Wigs

Laurie Freeman,
Peter Kufluk
Production Assistants

Charly Avni, Myra Malley,
Cam More, Bill Pyke,
Reg Reynolds, Ted Ross,
Mac Thomas
Technical Assistants

Calvin G. Rand
President 1965–

Brian Doherty
Founder and first President

Paxton Whitehead
Artistic Director 1967–

Barry Morse
Artistic Director 1966

Andrew Allan
Artistic Director 1963–1965

Sean Mulcahy
Associate Director 1963–1965

Thomas B. Burrows
General Manager 1971–

Judith C. Hendry
Publicity Director 1969–

Muriel Sherrin
General Manager 1968–1971

Raymond Wickens
*Company Manager and
Publicity Director 1965–1968*